Little Things That Keep Families Together

Little Things That Keep Families Together

Arline Cate Thrash

Broadman Press, Nashville, Tennessee

©Copyright 1976 ● Broadman Press.

All rights reserved.

4256-17

ISBN: 0-8054-5617-1

Unless otherwise indicated, all Scripture quotations are from the Revised Standard Version. Quotations marked (TLB) are from *The Living Bible, Paraphrased* (Wheaton: Tyndale House Publishers, 1971) and are used by permission.

Subject Heading: FAMILY

Dewey Decimal Classification: 301.427

Library of Congress Catalog Card Number: 76-24116

Printed in the United States of America

To Willard

Husband Extraordinary

Who Dared to Honor My Dreams

PREFACE

The cobwebs of time are spun of little things—earthy, mundane happenings.

"Mother, will they have a Chore Chart in heaven?"

"I bet God doesn't have to tote the garbage out every morning!"

"Mother, will this be another one of your woman's minutes?"

Centuries ago on a Judean hillside, Jesus reminded his disciples, "Let the children come to me, and do not hinder them; for to such belongs the kingdom of heaven" (Matt. 19:14). Perchance the kingdom has a very low door.

The kingdom of heaven here on earth belongs to these little ones who enter our homes and corral our hearts. Too soon they grow and go—like the melting of winter snow or the brush of butterfly wings on a summer night.

Fragile, shimmering moments we've shared with Douglas, Diane, Mark, and David are etched in memory's tapestry along with remembrances of our larger family on earth.

Arline Cate Thrash

CONTENTS

PART I: Meditations About Home

Whither Thou Goest 13
My Cup Runneth Over 14
Mama, Your Majesty, What's to Eat? 17
Such an Exciting Life 18
I Didn't Tell 19
Will I Fail Sunday School 20
Boquet for Bluebird 21
Nothing to Do but Be Good 23
What's in the Bottom of the Machine? 24
I Want to Be Helpless 25
Did God Forget to Hang Out the Sun? 26
Burden or Blessing 27
Just a Mama Now 28
Yes, No, or Wait Awhile 31
Mothers Do Mend 32
Which One Belongs to Me? 33
Every Family Needs a Mollie 35
"Mother, You're the Most!" 38
The House Hasn't Caught on Fire . . . 39
Tranquilizers for the Brood 40
I'm not Your Pal 41
"Mama" 42
Ode to a Vanishing Bank Account 43
I Resign 44
Blessings in Disguise 46
Rich in Everything but Money 47
One Way to Leave the Hospital 48
Good Morning, God 50

Now I Understand   51
When Can I Be a Teenager?   53
Aren't Memories Wonderful?   55

PART II: My Larger Family

World, Here I Come   59
Mother's Over the Hill—to Grad School   61
Hank Is Human   63
Bless This Roast   68
Our Martha   69
You Believed in Me!   72
Ode to Willard Et Ux, Et Al   73
My Friend Died Today   74
Invading a Sister Country   75
Houseswapping, Canadian Style   78
A Cup of Cold Water   81
Empty Nest Vaccine   83
He Was a Legend . . .   84
Confessions of Miz Lady   87
Nosegay to Granny   96
Hang in There   97
Ode to Pa Pa   100
William's Raise   101
Grandmother—Second Only to Solomon!   102
I Couldn't Pray   108
From Adam to Now   110

PART III: Emptying the Nest

Footfalls   115
Help! We're Outnumbered   116

Unexpected Bonus—The Joy Boys   117
To Our Plebe   120
"Dear Father"   125
Christmas Homecoming   126
New Home   127
Where Did My Little Girl Go?   129
"I Can't Pen a Poem"   130
Mom's Monstrosity   130
I Almost Threw in the Towel Today   132
Prayer for an Overextended Son   132
Driver's License   134
Learn to Nest in the Storm   135
Willy-nilly Nineteen!   136
Middlesence   138
When You Marry   140
Brothers in Christ   142
Middle Son's Graduation   143
Annapolis, 1974   144
Bless You, My Love   145
How Can I Know?   146
Beyond   149

Acknowledgments

"My Cup Runneth Over," page 14: From *Home Life*, December 1960. ©Copyright 1960, The Sunday School Board of the Southern Baptist Convention. All rights reserved. Used by permission.

"Just a Mama Now," page 28: From *Home Life*, July 1964. ©Copyright 1964, The Sunday School Board of the Southern Baptist Convention. All rights reserved. Used by permission.

"Grandmother, Second Only to Solomon!", page 102: From *Home Life*, October 1972. ©Copyright 1972, The Sunday School Board of the Southern Baptist Convention. All rights reserved. Used by permission.

Part 1
Meditations About Home

Teach them to your children. Talk
about them when you are sitting at home,
when you are out walking, at bedtime, and
before breakfast!

WHITHER THOU GOEST

Love knocked gently at my heart's door in the form of a long lanky athlete. I considered it only a wonderful friendship at first, but this young man had a very persuasive way about him. He declared his intentions three weeks after our first date. Then he set out on a campaign that put all other suitors in the shade! By summer's end if he had asked me to cross the Sahara on a geriatric camel, I would have attempted it. Some seventeen months later—my father believed in long engagements—I stood by the side of this lanky fellow on a New Years' night and promised whither he wentest, I would go.

I still feel a tinge of excitement at the sight of this tall, impractical guy with the green eyes who gave me wild mink for our second anniversary although we had no bedroom furniture.

Love and laughter, heartbreak, critical illnesses, a business collapse, floods, near fatal accidents, and a few hurricanes have enlivened our "whither thou goest!"

Were he to announce tomorrow we would be departing on a cattle boat for Australia, I'd be on the dock by daybreak with offspring and a few barrels of dishes.

When I hear eighteen-year-olds wail, "I've been going to college for a whole semester and haven't found a husband yet!" I marvel at how wonderfully uncomplicated by husband-hunting expeditions my dark-age days had been. I had no idea I was being deprived of so much anguish!

And I only wish the pendulum would swing back in the direction of the dark ages when man, the pursuer, mapped out his campaign for a maid and she enjoyed being courted, cherished, and committed in that order.

"I take you as my wife. I will love you, I will trust you, I will honor you whether we are together or apart. I will be your earthly sustaining force whether we are rich or even if we're broke, when we are healthy or even more should we be ill. I will be at your side giving you my strength, and together we will face the world as *one* united by God."

MY CUP RUNNETH OVER

Only a decade ago my husband and I met when we were both staffers at Ridgecrest, North Carolina. We climbed mountains, dreamed dreams, and at summer's end, with the sure confidence of the young, decided we had found our future in each other.

Now—ten years later—we find much grace is needed to be the caretakers of three young lads, one lone girl, a too small house, an aged station wagon, and more month than money left over. Our lack of wealth has been offset by a good sense of humor, but even that wears thin at times.

We have lived in four different states, and in nine apartments or houses. Yet, we've found that happiness is found not in houses large or small. It is carried within.

We have known times of plenty and other times have wondered from whence our daily bread was coming. Somehow, through each experience God has worked good for us even though we didn't always realize it at the time. Through the years we have discovered for ourselves lasting truth in the promise, "We know that all things work together for good to them that love God, to them who are called according to his purpose" (Rom. 8:28).

My husband is quite sure we could mint a small fortune when I get around to publishing my recipes for ground beef and leftover leftovers. Not that there are many leftovers anymore with three boys who seem to have bottomless pits for stomachs.

Anyone seeing my weekly grocery cart groaning under its heavy load could believe I was feeding an army or running a boarding house. Each time the milk bill arrives, we feel the urge to go in search of at least one healthy cow who digs little boys. Last Easter my husband brought me a large barbecued ham. When I ventured to suggest that most men remembered their wives with a posey instead of a ham, he said he knew of no better gift for a wife with a hungry family. Besides, he explained, he wanted me to enjoy my Sunday out of the kitchen. Secretly, I think he was evening the score on those huge red onions in his Christmas stocking.

I have never won any blue ribbons at the fair for my New Orleans spaghetti recipe, but it has made the rounds of many southern cities and has been consumed by thirty-six adults at a sitting without nary a complaint. My five-year-old Diane thinks I'm the best "cooker" in the whole world. Three-year-old Mark tells me he enjoyed his breakfast no matter what the meal happens to be. Our two-year-old eats anything I put on the table, especially if it happens to be on his brother's plate.

One of the family funnies concerns some frozen rolls I bought because I had no time to make any. They collapsed and spread it all over the pan. My husband announced I had no trouble with homemade rolls—just store-bought ones.

Another day I made a huge chocolate cake to take to an ailing friend. When I went to get the cake from its cooling place, I found the neighbor's dog had devoured the whole thing, waxed paper included. I have the reputation of being the only housewife on our block who bakes for friendly hounds.

Our house is furnished throughout in early matrimonial. Often we gaze at our good wing chair and a beautiful table lamp for which we paid twenty-five dollars in a moment of happy insanity. We've reconciled ourselves to the fact that when we are able to match these pieces, they'll be worn out or we will! Our one luxury, besides the dishwasher, is a stereo set with matching speakers. My husband gave me the choice between it and one-day-a-week help. I've regretted my decision only a few times when I eyed the set and wished it would get up and wax the floors or wash the windows.

In spite of our child-proof furnishings, our home has always been a favorite gathering place for old and young. When we were first married and lived in but two rooms, our pastor and friends of many backgrounds were welcome guests. In the years since, our guest book has included friends the world over who have shared a meal or found lodging in our home. In whatever city we're transferred, we count on our church to widen our circle of friendship with those who share similar goals.

Life has been far from Pollyanna perfect! We have not been spared our share of pain and misfortune. Many times one or both of us has been ready to give up. Other times we have been physically unable to pray. A daily practice of reading God's Word together and praying has brought us through innumerable crises.

All four of our children have been born prematurely because of a broken back I sustained during my college days.

I've spent weeks in traction before and after childbirth. "Be still and know that I am God" is a reality in my life, not a far-fetched promise. Our youngest sons had bronchial asthma since birth, and we have waited endless days and nights as they lay under oxygen tents with collapsed lungs. Each year when our business associates invest their bonus checks, ours goes to repay loans incurred by heavy medical expenses. Yet, this makes the lives of our children more precious. When the youngest ones sing "Into My Heart" at bedtime, it has a meaning all its own. Sometimes my husband jests that he has invested so much in me I must live to be at least ninety so he can finish paying for me.

My youthful dreams of doing something great have dissolved into more mature purposes. To impart to our children the spiritual and cultural heritage my parents gave to me, along with their common sense and gifted sense of humor, will take a lifetime of my cup overflowing!

MAMA, YOUR MAJESTY, WHAT'S TO EAT?

Eating is the children's favorite occupation. "Eat it before it eats you" is their motto! When I hear of mothers actually giving their offspring prescriptions to improve their appetites, I'm absolutely amazed. We just try to get ours to stop occasionally! They're the only kids in the neighborhood with a built-in radar system which detects brownies breathing in the oven four blocks away.

Were I to put a bale of fodder on the table, I believe our sons would dig in and attack it without question. It did take some vigorous training, but they would never think of leaving the table without expressing gratitude for whatever appeared on the scene. Once Mark, seated at another table in a restaurant, came over to ask if he could please be excused. Had I seen him carting his dishes to the kitchen, I wouldn't have been too surprised! (This son always makes up the beds in the motel so people won't think we're lazy and folds his napkin back immaculately so they can use it again.)

When dinner guests came one evening, the youngest one left the table to explore the toy box. David brought him back by the cuff of his neck. "Yu don't leave this table without xcusing yourself and telling my mudder yu enjoyed it whuther you did er not!"

Life is so daily we often forget these small courtesies that add zest to the home front. Sometimes all three sons rush over to seat me even though we're only having hamburgers. At such high moments I realize it's not nearly so important what you eat as the atmosphere in which you eat it. Once Mark got carried away with a cake recipe. "Mother, would you show my someday wife how to stir that one up?"

"Son, if you're wise, you'll never bring up the subject with your someday wife! You have a few things yet to learn."

"Man shall not live by bread lone," quote the boys. "It takes cookies and Kool-Aid, too!"

SUCH AN EXCITING LIFE

"Batten down" had been the dreaded cry for many hours! It was now 2 A.M. and *Cleo* in womanly fury, had just collapsed the Miami weather tower with winds of over 120 miles per hour. The malaluka tree had split open and toppled to the ground; a flying saucer of aerial debris thudded on the roof with ear-splitting snorts. Our house was vibrating and the plumbing was rumbling and groaning. We had put the children to bed for the fourth time. As we huddled in bed wondering which would go first—the roof, foundation, or the whole works, our Diane flew back into the bedroom and flung her arms about me.

"Oh, Mother, I just want you to know that if we are blown to heaven tonight, I've had such an exciting ten years! I've been to one wedding, two funerals, and now a hurricane!"

Such absolute faith in our heavenly Father's protective powers no matter what happened could only come from one so young.

The hurricane continued to rage outside, but peace settled upon our four walls. "Acquaint now thyself with him, and be at peace" (Job 23:21, KJV).

I DIDN'T TELL

Breathes there a parent who doesn't emotionally accompany each child on his first day of school? Anxiously our household awaited a blow-by-blow account of that magic day from our firstborn. We heard him before we saw him.

"Motheer! We didn't learn to read today, but guess what?"

I gave up on the first try.

"Oh, Mother! (gales of laughter) We have the biggest, fattest teacher! She is so funny. You ought to see her squashing the desks together to get up and down the rows. And she doesn't break any speed records, either! He then gave an academy award-winning performace of this feat to his captivated audience of brothers and a sister.

Horrified at the thought of this very honest son mentioning his teacher's obesity, I ventured, "Douglas, you didn't tell your teacher she was too fat, did you?"

Pondering a moment, he flashed those immense, deep-set eyes. "Oh, no ma'm. I didn't tell her. I figured she knew it already so I just kept it to myself!"

There are many things we should leave unsaid and keep to ourselves. Stinging, sarcastic words that scratch and scar. Giving someone a piece of our mind when we have none to spare. Harsh, abrasive faultfinding, using the feeble excuse: "I'm telling you this for your own good" Others know their faults with no prompting from us. Insinuations. "Isn't it too bad that . . . ." And we're off and going! Half-truths. "I don't mean to gossip, but is it true that . . . ?

How do I know this? I am guilty. My mother had a very wise rule. "Don't tell everything you know. Save some of it." That parent tape replays within me often.

"Set a watch over your words." Before we share that juicy tidbit or seek to build ourselves by rubbing the glitter off another's crown, we need to pause and ask ourselves: Is it true? Is it necessary? Will it help the situation?

WILL I FAIL SUNDAY SCHOOL?

Just before the yearly "Commotion Day," as our children called it, David became quite worried. "Daddy, do you think I'll be promoted? I sure don't want to fail Sunday School!"

As I reflected on the young adult women I taught in Bible study, I knew two or three of them had actually failed Sunday School. God had given them so many blessings, including excellent health and wonderful husbands. Yet, these young mothers were indifferent or careless, feeling little or no responsibility in training their little ones or returning any part of God's gift.

Before becoming too critical or superimposing my

self-righteous moral diagnosis on my friends, I turned my thoughts inward. How easily we magnify others' faults and minimize our own! God had never failed me or gone back on a single promise. How permanent are his promises! Yet, how often I'd grieved him and failed him. I'd become earthbound, clay-footed, unproductive, weighed down with things that really didn't matter as I wandered through the airless rooms of daily existence. Unprepared, I'd barged into his presence, demanding like a spoiled child instead of seeking, handing him my time schedule. "I'd like this by tomorrow noon, but if you're terribly busy, I could wait until tomorrow night!"

How I've grieved the Holy Spirit with my immaturity, my selfishness. How I've tried his patience. But he's never given up or abandoned me. There are no inadequacies in him. Worthy is the Lamb!

This Galilean is too much for our small hearts! Help me to remove self from dead center, and let you take over. Talk for me, react for me, and love through me.

BOUQUET FOR BLUEBIRD

For years I've read of ads telling where to send baby's first shoes to have them preserved in bronze, and where to send old rugs or fur coats to be made into new creations. But never have I read a satisfactory recycling tidbit on what to do with aged, broken-down station wagons that are part of a family's history.

This bit of research occurred recently when my husband dropped a domestic bombshell by announcing the trade-off of Old Bluebird.

"What? Trade off Bluebird!" I cried out in disbelief.

"Why that's just like trading off one of the family!" Which sounded like a wonderful idea since all four had been sick with an assortment of asthma, flu, and tonsillitis.

"Just because Bluebird has 75,000 miles, a half-burned clutch, faulty brakes, an oil leak, and seldom starts in rainy weather, is that any reason to cast her aside? What will the boys do for entertainment when we no longer bump and jerk down the road to the accompanying tune of all those grinding noises?"

I knew by that certain fatal look in my honey's eye that I was fighting a losing battle so I began to reminisce of the six years she had been in our custody.

It was the last day of May when my husband drove down that small friendly lane in Memphis, Tennessee, in that gorgeous Bluebird. All our neighbors were present to witness the joyous happening. Had my husband driven up in a chariot with six horses, he wouldn't have been more impressive.

I arose at six the next morning to peep outside and reaffirm the fact that I was not dreaming. Learning to drive it under husbandly tutelage with two wee passengers is a recollection I hope never to conjure up from the back burner of my medulla.

Two sons and three states later Bluebird became mine as my husband gave up and bought a secondhand disaster that would not be littered with kids, used chewing gum, battered books, half-eaten apples, and second or thirdhand tissues.

We were quite a sight as we rolled down the road, usually with a couple of spares. One morning in the shopping center an elderly gentleman gaped in dumbfoundment as seven lively ones tumbled out the back tailgate of prodigious Bluebird. He was aghast when daughter sweetly announced, "Oh, we left three at home!"

I lived at the end of the line, in more ways than one, and always seemed to be the elected one to pick up and deliver all the children. Oftentimes I would have gladly invested in a pair of earplugs or six or seven muzzles.

One summer while my better half was in school in upstate New York, I drove over three thousand miles with our brood; I could have applied for a chauffeur's citation. After my husband's schooling, we moved to the city of his birth. It was here he announced before the last leaf fell from our trees, Bluebird's motor would surely fall out.

I have asked to absent myself from our abode when they carry away Bluebird. And so I pen this wee tribute con amore to my aged chariot which has seen me through so many of life's memorable moments. Were there a heaven for old cars, Bluebird would be right there in the front ranks wearing a crooked halo and a half-eaten peanut butter sandwich. Who knows? There might even be a leftover child spilling out the back tailgate!

NOTHING TO DO BUT BE GOOD

The spring monsoons had arrived bringing mildewy tempers. After three days of nothing but rain and more rain, daughter Diane padded softly into the kitchen and asked in a wee, wistful voice, "Mother, is there anything to do but be good?" I chuckled as my motherly instinct told me those dishes could wait.

I blushed as I thought how very like my daughter I was. How often I blundered into his presence asking the same question. Someone was always arriving on my doorstep needing to be cheered up when my problems were far greater. I was the village Mother McCree with children spilling from every corner. After all, when you have four of your own, a few more won't matter. Or so my friends thought! Never a week went by without a goodwill wagon run, delivering goodies to shut-ins. How come nobody ever thought I needed cheering up?

Tears splashed on notepaper as I tried to pen a cheery note to someone ill or discouraged. Was there no end to this? Didn't anyone realize I became exasperated and ready to kick life in the teeth?

After my foolish bouts of self-pity and impatience, I paused to thank my Father that someone did need me. God created me to know divine discontent and restlessness that could only be satisfied when I forgot self and reached out to others. I was truly my happiest at these times.

One of the strangest paradoxes of human experience is that he who gives himself away most completely has more of himself to give. And no matter how hard you try, you can't outgive God.

WHAT'S IN THE BOTTOM OF THE MACHINE?

On those rare occasions when life becomes almost dull, I can always gain new perspective by washing a load of clothes and looking on the bottom of the washer. Treasures there remind me again of the wondrous, carefree world of children and help restore partial lucidity.

Most mothers in their right mind would empty all those jean pockets before calling the repairman for the third time. Had I done this, I would have deprived myself of finding Doug's precious piece of quartz which he had heaved all the way from the Smoky Mountains. Or Mark's tooth, complete with the $7 filling, which he had so carefully hoarded to sell to this younger brother for the tooth fairy. A sand castle in the bottom of the washer almost undid me.

A mound of waterlogged raisins led me to the culprit who had violated the rule of carrying food to other parts of the house. Said culprit accused me of having eyes in the back of my head, never realizing that the machine had done my detective work! Once I located a precious audit slip for which my husband had searched the house in vain. Our youngest was delighted to have his dollar bill wet-cleaned. I became quite cautious for a week or so after two giant crayons escaped my detection and melted on a load of white clothes! The jolly of the decade, to everyone but Mom, came when we lived in a cramped seminary apartment and a large box of instant mashed potato flakes toppled off the shelf right into the machine! A collector's dime, worth $15, turned up in the lint trap.

Equally strange are the unexpected treasures of life. We weary ourselves in the pursuit of pleasure, happiness, and the good life in far-off places when the treasure lies in quite ordinary places and events. After exhausting our resources in a vain search, we find—quite by accident—that happiness is a by-product, and radiant good cheer comes from forgetting self and serving others. What a priceless discovery!

I WANT TO BE HELPLESS

Bursting through the kitchen door at dusk, Diane panted, "Please, Mother, tell me what I can do for you. I want to be helpless!"

How many times I've been helpless to another human being in need. Helpless because my faith was too small, my day too busy, or my judgments too pronounced. In short, I didn't really care enough. Love—God's kind—is unconditional, uncalculating, and nonjudgmental. It asks not, nor dwells upon the question of worthiness. "Simon, I have something to say to you. . . . Her sins—and they are many—are forgiven."

Jesus never rushed up to people and confronted them with their sins. He never hurried. Rather he walked calmly, quietly beside people listening to their problems with deep sensitivity. He did not interrupt. Is it any wonder so many responded and were made totally whole? He saw situations through their eyes, their senses! He met them exactly where they were, wasting no time debating how they managed to get into any predicament. How natural for a little lad's father to confess excitedly, "I do have faith; oh, help me to have more!"

Take my too-small faith and multiply it like the mustard seed. I do want to help, to bear, and share. For sharing is the hallmark of gratitude.

DID GOD FORGET TO HANG OUT THE SUN?

A predawn drizzle was falling on New Orleans, the city of sin and shopping. Suddenly David tripped into the bedroom, peered through the curtains at the gloomy beginning, then scooted over to our bed, thudded me on the cheeks, and shouted, "Wake up, Mudder, wake up and look! God forgot to hang out the sun today!"

I smiled sleepily at his young logic, but his words returned to haunt me. Just how many times in the past months had I in essence accused God of forgetting to hang out the sun? Had I not told my dearest friend I was going to light a few flares to remind him of our whereabouts?

God had performed painful, spiritual surgery on our lives. We had known cleansing fires in which he'd refined us and reshaped our destiny. This had been a costly process as our wills, our hearts, and our fortunes were broken before God could deal with us. It took these heart scalds to make us realize our heavenly Father makes no mistakes, and we must allow him to be God in every circumstance. What a costly lesson! Throughout it all we were humbled and strengthened as we claimed firsthand his wonderful promise, "When you pass through the waters I will be with you; and through the rivers, they shall not overwhelm you . . . for I am the Lord your God" (Isa. 43:2-3).

"No, son," I thought. "God didn't forget. And he needs no flares to know our whereabouts! His sun is still shining.

BURDEN OR BLESSING

"Hey, Mother, how 'bout giving this essay the 'ole English eagle eye so I can get on with earning this next rank?" boomed Mark.

The first sentence was really an attention getter! "I tithe because I have to, not because I want to." Horrified at first, I burst into laughter. This was our very honest son!

Ever since the children had been able to hold ten shiny brown pennies in their grubby little fists, they seemed to latch onto the concept that God deserved the first one. Or had they? Maybe this was wistful thinking on the part of Mom and Dad. At our family devotion that evening we talked about God's wonderful gifts and the children named some, including the cat and a baby squirrel which had expired and been given a fitting burial. We shared experiences of the joys of returning to God a small bit of all he'd given us. "Now that doesn't mean the money will really roll in or you'll become a millionaire. It does mean that God will take care of your needs. . . ." "I guess we get our needs and greeds mixed up, don't we, Daddy?"

Will a man rob God? No, man robs himself of what he could be, could do if he took God at his word. God's gifts never wear out, and he will pour out spiritual blessings far beyond our expectations. Only man with his limited vision sets a ceiling on these blessings. God has no closed shop. In every need he is previous.

You can have as much of God as you can hold.

JUST A MAMA NOW

The day was warm and lazy, one that makes a Louisiana siesta so inviting. I was trying to unglue both eyes at once and at the same time rationalizing that the ironing would really keep another day in the freezer. Suddenly there were muffled voices beneath my window.

"You know, my mother doesn't get up and go to work like she used to. She just teaches us. I guess you'd say she's just a mama now," Mark informed his buddy.

Precious words from a proud six-year-old to his chum. For two long years I'd combined the roles of wife, mother, teacher, family bookkeeper, and caretaker of a far too small apartment on a graduate campus. As my physical stamina waxed dim and dreams of South Sea Islands where kids wore no clothes overtook me, I was certain we were the only couple who'd ever reached the spry old age of thirty before realizing a little learning is a dangerous thing.

My husband thought of inventing an eight-day week. We never seemed to get through in seven! He was tied with another student for having the most part-time jobs. During our two-year stay he worked as a night guard on a construction site, a cashier in a nearby department store, a high school

Latin and glee club instructor, night clerk in a motel, and minister of music at a suburban church. His mother often teased him that one day he might have enough education to dig ditches! I taught the mechanics of English to many unwilling scholars in a private school in New Orleans by day and came home to my own night school.

Our house took on that certain "lived-in look," and I took on a "caved-in, washed out" appearance as I transported mounds of soggy laundry to groaning clotheslines, packed six lunches nightly, ironed every other day, reigned as the kitchen queen, and wondered when I was to take time out to live.

My sweet husband still retained his boyhood talent of bringing home anyone who looked the least bit hungry. Douglas, a wise old-ten-year-old, sensed my futility on this score and assured me he would never do his wife like that if he ever got him one. I almost wept as I was sure to be long departed before this event took place.

In the late summer I was stricken with a serious infection which I was unable to throw off because of pernicious anemia. Two weeks later I collapsed from blood loss. As is true with most crises, my husband was far removed from the city. We always wait until he departs before falling headfirst out of trees, catching toes in the lawnmower, or being bitten by a monkey who liked us better than the banana.

Three months of enforced rest, daily medication, and constant threat of major surgery made me about as much help to my husband as Lady Job had been to hers! Financial strain was added to the problem of regained health, but my husband took on extra employment instead of becoming a quitter.

In the early morning hours when pain jackknifed through my whole being and sleep was impossible, I wondered along with Job and countless others, "Oh, that I knew where I might find him." For months I had fought the battle, as had all toiling wives, yes, with time—our unseen enemy. Suddenly I had time, for the body heals on its own schedule. A blessing is in this storm somewhere. Don't let me escape it.

Hadn't our children been a real joy to us during our "Getting Daddy Thru School"? Each had made his bed since age three and all shared in housekeeping responsibilities. How many times had Doug admonished me to get to bed by nine? "I'll scrub up the kitchen and put the troops to bed!" And he had—bless him. Remember the time he accidentally knocked that box of instant potatoes out of the storage cabinet right into the washing machine. Or the night Diane introduced her new international neighbor: "Mama, did you know Tricia lived right next door to an interrupted volcano?" We'd enjoyed our little here far more than our much elsewhere. The children's eyes shown like black diamonds at the sight of an occasional ice cream double-decker, an unexpected bag of donuts, or the end of the month McDonald Special.

On a November 30, I was released by my doctor and given permission to resume teaching following many soup bone (more bone than soup) and "red bean and rice" days.

When the strain of grad school plus two full-time-part-time jobs, a bushed wife, and four boisterous kids became too much, my husband threatened to spend a few peaceful hours snoring in the demonstration bedroom of the nearest department store. A good laugh at ourselves cleared the air and avoided clashes of tired tempers.

Winter gave up, spring skipped along, and graduation day finally arrived. All of us, including my husband's parents and my mother, went to get "Daddy's Diploma." As he proudly received the handshake of the president, there was no doubt in the minds of any nearby whose daddy that was! Our David, scheduled to graduate from kindergarten on the same day asked wistfully if he could wear his graduation suit (a white cap and gown) to Daddy's graduation.

And here I am—just a mama now—reading daily to my children, speaking broken Spanish and fractured French to them, doctoring simple cuts, and doling out the comfort cookie. One forgets these daily joys until they cease to be!

Would we repeat our school-after-thirty experience? Yes, a thousand times yes! Despite feeding, clothing, and keeping four in shoes. What friendships! Nightly our boys pray for their good buddy in Mexico. "Do you think we should pray for him in Spanish? Would it get there faster?" Paul and his family should be doubly blessed if little boys' prayers count. And they do!

God's grace has no favorite location. It can't be confined; it is all sufficient anywhere. And I claim his every promise to "just a mama!"

"She will not hinder him but help him all her life."

YES, NO, OR WAIT AWHILE

Very ladylike our daughter was explaining prayer to a neighbor as she helped her hang out sheets on a wind-whipped clothesline. Diane loves to help the neighbors!

"God answers prayer in three different ways at least. Sometimes he just surprises us and says yes outright. Other times he says no just like a parent! But sometimes he says wait awhile, you're not ready to have that prayer answered."

What childish wisdom! When my heavenly Father answers yes, the real test lies just ahead. What will I do with his gift—use it or abuse it?

And why should I puff up when God's answer is no. How often as a parent have I refused a childish request, knowing it would bring harm, not good. God will not grant a request that would hurt another, cripple my potential, or compromise my finest self. How much more God knows about me, his earthling, than I know about myself. When I set the terms for him, am I not trying to manipulate him as my children do me? Why do I go on limiting God's power within me by assuming such a childish attitude?

Often I chafe under God's wait awhile. I want him to adopt my time schedule, not his! In fact, I've figured out all the angles for him; all he need do is sign the blank check. How often I cheat myself and become totally disillusioned because I expect God to do things a certain way—my way! And he doesn't.

When I tire of doing God's homework for him and acknowledge him as Creator and I the created, his time comes and the gift is granted. It may not be what I requested, but his gift is far superior to anything I dared ask for, hope for, or dream about! When will I cease to argue, speculate, debate, justify, or theorize?

"Oh, the unexplored reminders of God! Who ever saw his last star?"

MOTHERS DO MEND

We felt a strange kinship to Father Abraham as we set out on a thousand-mile journey into the unknown. From the coast of Louisiana to the city of Miami seemed as distant as the Ur of the Chaldees. Looking at our chariot overflowing with children and cargo, I felt all we lacked were a train of camels and a few dozen servants, both of which would have come in quite handy.

We had chosen the coastal route along the Gulf. On the first day we allowed the children to go up to water's edge while we hiked over to a small grocery. All fatherly admonitions of avoiding the water were quickly forgotten, and two parents returned to find all four offspring waist-deep in the Gulf of Mexico! Discipline was administered to the seat of reason and was worsened by wet clothing! However, I detected that certain twinkle in my husband's eye which told me that if he had faced the same temptation, he would have reacted exactly as his offspring did.

By the third day of the scenic route, my husband was sinking fast from too much togetherness! Alas, it was I who listened to all that off-key singing, squabbling, made-up jollies and riddles, squabbling, happy commotion, squabbling. Came the blessed darkness and my better half trudged up and down the beach alone, gladly exchanging the pounding surf for the typhoon of cooped-up fatherhood.

Our eldest sensed the strain of the evening. Just before bedtime while Father was still trudging, eldest called out, "Cheer up, Madre! I know you feel like an overhaul is needed, but you'll be almost as good as new in a few days. After all, Mothers do mend!"

Shortly thereafter, my otherness returned—shoes and socks in hand and soaking wet from the waist down!

Oft times when the malady of motherhood overtakes me, I remember that mothers do mend. God, in infinite wisdom, gave mothers marvelous recuperative powers.

WHICH ONE BELONGS TO ME?

Family reunions with all my husband's kissin' kin are more entertaining than a child's first circus. Grandma Davis, the matriarch of the clan who lived to be ninety-four, presided over the happy bedlam which began early on Mother's Day morn in her big Mississippi country yard. By dinner time the show had spilt over to the school yard across the gravel road.

Stingy emotions were unheard of in this clan. Relatives fell upon one another, hugging and weeping for joy. Our sons became quite adept at dodging all that emoting but only daughter received more squeezes than the Charmin!

There was no such thing as a meat boycott; we could have edited "101 Different Ways to Devour Chicken." Young and old ate like dropouts from six weeks of Weight Watchers.

My husband's aunts and his mother looked very much alike, especially with their starched-up beehive hairdos. As the early afternoon pitch of excitement grew higher and higher, a puzzled Mark kept gazing at all those look-alike sisters. Finally he edged up timidly to his Grandpa, nudged him, and whispered into his ear, "Pa Pa, which one of those grannies belongs to me?"

All of us want to belong! To be somebody! Self-identity—the need to be recognized and affirmed, runs very deep. All children wear the sign, "I want to be important NOW!" Most of our problems arise because no one reads that sign.

Loss of identity is tragic. This identity, this sense of belonging doesn't come from expensive toys, living in the right neighborhood, country club membership, or indulgences galore! Security comes from being assured often by word and deed that you're loved, wanted, trusted, and respected. With these ingredients the foundation never trembles even though finances may be shaky. Coupled with this warmth, concern, and affection is fair-minded discipline. A child who has never been crossed is a very unhappy, insecure, and frustrated child! The old mountaineer who chortled, "I love 'em, I lick 'em, I believe in 'em," may not have been too far from right.

EVERY FAMILY NEEDS A MOLLIE

A family's first dog, like a lass's first love, is never quite forgotten! Our first dog was Mollie, half collie, half German shepherd, and she came straight from the city dog pound at the tender age of three months and two feet! Her owner had carried her and two kinfolk to the shelter since he could no longer afford to feed them. After she began devouring everything in sight, I wondered which I could afford—Mollie or three sons.

We acquired Mollie on my birthday; the children wanted to get me something different that year. Believe me, it was! Actually, Mark longed for a horse to tether under his bunk bed, but the shelter was fresh out of horses. He declared that Mollie belonged the moment he laid eyes on her. She had the color of a collie, the size and features of a German shepherd, and her big soulful brown eyes equaled those of eldest son. Sitting between all three boys—a feat only a dog can accomplish—Mollie shivered and whined all the way home despite reassurances from the boys.

The minute we pulled into the driveway, her listlessness was a thing of the past. She leaped from the wagon and chased every dog, cat, car, and people in the neighborhood. Eldest and I spent the afternoon sprinting hedges and hurdling flowerbeds to return Mollie to home base. Long after dark one Daddy returned to find a Mollie happily panting on the screened front porch and a Mom unhappily panting on the living room couch.

"Now, honey, you ought to know! Dogs, like children, are not trained overnight." He digested those very words several times!

A true Southern dog, Mollie inhaled rice and gravy, black-eyed peas, sweet potatoes, and her favorite treat was pancakes dripping with syrup. We had to coax her to eat all that newfangled dog food, and the children ate twice as many dog biscuits as she.

In a family conference, where certain parents resorted to mild brainwashing tactics, it was decided 15 to 4 that Mollie would not be allowed to roam the house. As I made my way up Mount Everest with the daily tons of laundry, I heard Mollie galloping up and down all three flights to the delightful war whoops of our youngest cowboys. Her favorite reclining spot was in the middle of daughter's bed. A very refined dog, she always picked up the pink rug and placed it on the bed before she closed the door and settled down to her siesta. One rainy evening when we smelled spring but winter still lingered, I came down Everest to find dog and Dad stretched before a crackling fire. Both were fast asleep.

The oldest were up at dawn to gallop Mollie on her first stroll; they resented having to go off to school and leave Mollie to the care of the "little boys." David, at three, and Mollie were inseparable; he creaked down the long sidewalk on his trike (I never oiled it as the squeak was my radar-tracking system) with Mollie in tow. When people asked him what kind of dog he had, he solemnly announced, "She's a Mollie, and we got her at the dog pound!" That put us in a class all our own since we lived in an older, established neighborhood where everybody owned pedigrees with papers two miles long!" She wasn't much of a dog according to neighborhood standards. All the other dogs could perform tricks galore. Not Mollie! When told to stand on her hind legs, she'd just as soon flop over in a five-minute coma. If the boys commanded her to play dead, she'd spring into instant action.

Before many days Mollie managed to push out the lower screen section of our Civil War monstrosity so she could gallop in without wasting time for the door to be opened. The next day we noticed the younger ones entering Mollie style. This became habit for all three. One day out-of-town friends watched in dumbfounded fascination as dog and kids raced through on all fours. "Shall we enter the same way?" they inquired.

As Mollie became older, she could not resist the temptation to chase cars when the children were inside or occupied otherwise. We lived on a busy triangle corner and my husband spent more than one afternoon driving around the triangle, waiting for Mollie to chase his car. She didn't disappoint him! He would get out, grab her, and swat her behind the ears with a rolled-up newspaper. "This doesn't hurt her nearly so much as it scares her," he would explain. However, I noticed the kids kept their distance when Daddy picked up the newspaper!

Mollie's continuing car-chasing sport and a near-fatal accident to our youngest resulted in our having to find a new home for Mollie. We were at the hospital day and night followed by weeks of schedule readjustments so I found a new home for Mollie in the country with four little boys.

Our last glimpse of Mollie was a reassuring one even though the children refused to be reassured. Mollie was wedged between all four boys in an ancient wagon, mournfully munching the buttons off their shirts. David, unable to walk for many days, cried all afternoon. "I'm not ever gonna be happy again as they taked away my Mollie!" The family left their phone number and just before dusk we called so all could hear Mollie bark. Mollie was the solo of the bedtime prayers, and Daddy came home to find all of us bawling.

Five years and other pets have passed. Each time I see a dilapidated screen door, bittersweet memories rush forth. Life with Mollie was as short-lived as many a first love, and just as intense. As the youngest son says, "Every family needs a Mollie!"

" MOTHER, YOU'RE THE MOST!"

The day had been at least thirty hours long. Tempers were skating on thin ice and patience was not a virtue to be reckoned with at this stage in the game. I'd given Mark and David their final warning—silence and a look that reminded them of the sky before the thunderstorm. Mama's "You're Walking on Eggshells Stare," as Douglas aptly termed it.

Despite this, our monsters were getting their fifty-fourth drink of the night. They disarmed me completely by marching into the kitchen, where I was sinking at too rapid a rate, and giving me a snappy salute and a timid, boyish near miss of a hug. "Mother, you're the most!" they exclaimed. I had no earthly idea of what I was the most of and they did not elaborate, having used up their last chance at the water cooler. All conjured up threats died on my lips that night!

"A word fitly spoken is like apples of gold in pictures of silver." Truly my sons' words were this. How adept we are at forgetting to speak encouraging words in our home; we simply take for granted those who love us most. The home is the most difficult place to live like Jesus because our family knows us far too well! Yet if God can't use us in our own home, there is less likelihood of his using us outside of it. I recommend Jesus to my children by the life I live and the example I set as a mother. Such a sobering truth sends me to my prayer closet daily.

I'm reminded of this each evening as I hold forth in the pandemonium of a too-small kitchen with three whirlwinds spilling forth and a fourth screeching on his cello in the most distant room possible. I may be the first woman in history driven from home by a cello rendition (the word means to tear apart) of "Mary Had a Little Lamb."

Life is made up of just such moments spiced by a few "Mother, You're the Most" memories embroidered in the skeins of motherhood.

THE HOUSE HASN'T CAUGHT ON FIRE . . .

Once we were the delightful caretakers of a three-story monstrosity. Since it appeared that Bluebeard had just vacated it, leaving all the skeletons in the attic, we named it "Gray Monster." On windswept nights when the shutters banged we could all but hear the eerie voices of Bluebeard's wives. The boys scooted up and down all those flights in sheer ecstacy, hauling deceased insects, rock collections, and empty medicine bottles. By dusk each evening those stairs looked like Mount Everest. I wondered why I continued to give those boys vitamins instead of swallowing them all myself! My bones creaked almost as loudly as the house but my spirits soared with the laughter and warmth of a young family. Each time the night wind blew shingles off the roof, the children would sneak up behind me and rasp their favorite spine-tingler, "Bluebeard is returning; who will be his next victim?" I figured the kids would get me long before Bluebeard! He wouldn't look at me twice.

Tragedy struck while we lived in the monster. We lost all our savings in an unsuccessful business partnership. Some weeks later our youngest son was in critical condition as the result of a freak accident, and he lay in a coma for endless hours. When the days of his recovery period stretched into weeks as he learned to use his leg muscles again, I realized my spiritual resources were bankrupt. I'd drawn on them too heavily; there was no reserve.

As I sat stargazing in the bay window seat, my spirit as bleak and barren as the windswept trees, our Mark crept up to me and whispered in my ear, "Mother, the house hasn't caught on fire yet!"

With timid words my small son had put the sun back in my sky. Is it small wonder our children learn joy, or its counterpart, despair, from us?

I, as a mother, set the emotional climate of my home each day. If I'm grouchy, it's contagious. No wonder the old mountaineer from Tennessee expounded, "If religion don't triumph over temperament, it ain't much good!"

TRANQUILIZERS FOR THE BROOD

My uncle's barnyard livened with drama on our children's first visit to a sure 'nuff farm. Boisterously they stormed the hen house, tumbled from the hayloft, and clambered over the railing of a real hog pen.

"Now I'm beginning to get the picture of the prodigal son," mused an excited Doug after watching a huge hog wallow in the mud. "Yes, and that hog's little brother wasn't doing badly!" another informed us.

Cautiously the children crept up to a duck pen and poked their fingers at the downy soft creatures. Off they flew, trying to catch a guinea! David gently nestled a wee calf, then cleared the fence at record speed with Papa Bull in hot pursuit!

"I'm not riding Queenie Horse again till I get a seat belt!"

So enraptured were they with the barnyard population, we actually had to call them three times to the evening meal. This was unheard of!

"Please warn me a few days before next year's visit so I can give my hens a few tranquilizers," my aunt bemoaned. "These hens will probably lay scrambled eggs in the morning!"

Fat as a pumpkin, an East Tennessee moon hovered over the hills as we drove through the gate and down a country lane. My aunt declares she heard the animals sigh with relief.

"A time to be born and a time to die;
   A time to plant, and a time to [harvest] . . ." (see Eccl. 3:2).

How very much our "city children" missed by never experiencing the earthy drama of life on a farm.

I'M NOT YOUR PAL

"I'm not your pal; I am your father. You will have many pals and peers throughout life but only one father. Don't ever forget that."

"You have only one childhood; don't waste it. Because you're young only once, you have only one chance to grow up to be a secure, responsible adult.

Harsh words from a father? I think not. As parents we have been mindful of the old adage, "Give me a child until he is seven." We've realized these tiny seedlings placed in our care would be ours for only a few short years. We could not arrest their development by making life too easy for them because childhood is the preparation period for living. We took seriously the biblical admonition that the eagle stirs up her nest that the young may learn to fly.

Children, like arrows, must be straightened and polished if they are to go straight to the point of duty and hit the mark. Otherwise they return to pierce the parents' hearts.

"Most of the time you will understand why I expect or demand certain things of you. However, there will be times when you don't understand, nor will you understand until you grow up and have children of your own. Not understanding doesn't excuse disobedience! Someone will hold authority over you all your life; rules are necessary."

My husband's formula is simplicity itself. "Never give an order unless it is necessary or beneficial and then *make it stick.*" In the midst of frequent growls of protest, he pursues his course calmly, firmly, with a touch of humor, never giving in for an instant to our carping critters. If there is parental discussion or disagreement, it takes place out of offsprings' hearing range.

One of the gravest mistakes of our generation of "depression children" is that so many become pampering parents, doling out to their kids everything they themselves did not have with no strings attached, never realizing that deprivation and delayed gratification are character-builders. A wise and wealthy matron, denied nothing, sadly mused, "I have missed something of immense value by never knowing the emotion of want."

In our so-called Golden Age of Gadgets, loving expectation is a scarce commotion in the marketplace. Undisciplined parents who practice no restraint or self-imposed responsibility can expect either undisciplined, unrestrained children or resentment-laden children who say in essence, "Live it before you demand it."

Imperfect as it is, our home is a lively training ground where children, like parents, can and do fail sometimes in a climate of acceptance. But expectation runs high. Again a gem from my husband. "If you expect nothing of your children, don't be too disappointed when they fulfill that expectation!"

The best way of expressing parental love is to prepare a child for the successful management of his life. Today's children will be tomorrow's builders of the Kingdom. God has no grandchildren!

"MAMA"

I know how tired you are.
So I just said a little prayer

for you.

To help you through tomorrow.
I love you SO MUCH!

>Diane

P. S. I hope you have a good sleep.

(found on my dresser one evening)

ODE TO A VANISHING BANK ACCOUNT

The car expired today. Too much loving neglect! No amount of heart massage or mouth-to-pocketbook resuciatation would revive that gas-guzzler. Last week the lawnmower self-destructed with a bit of help from two offspring who filled the gas tank with sand. Saturday morning right in the middle of "Bugs Bunny" and "Road Runner" the tube sank into an incurable coma. Shortly before sundown last Friday our arthritic, jaundiced stereo disintegrated after spewing sparks like a fire-eating dragon!

It's as if all these applicances were psychic and knew the very moment we managed to accumulate one dollar above the minimum balance allowed in our checking account! As the repairman philosophizes, "Lady, they don't make 'em to last fifty years anymore."

"Just think what would happen to our economy if they did!" I was thinking—about our vanishing account and wishing for the longevity of my mother's Maytag wringer which even outlived the coiled-topped G.E. refrigerator, the patriarch of all appliances.

"Do not toil to acquire wealth . . . . When your eyes light upon it, it is gone; for suddenly it takes to itself wings, flying like an eagle toward heaven" (Prov. 23:4-5). There wasn't the remotest danger of our ever acquiring wealth; it had winged swifter than an eagle into the unknown. I believe the Almighty in his wisdom knew the exact amount he could entrust to the Willard Thrashes, and he wasn't about to put a stumbling block in our pathway.

Things *don't* last. How transitory they are! Take money—somedays we have it; more often we owe it. Yet, my heart soars and sings as I realize we're rich in so many other areas! We have joy unspeakable and fantastic bounce-back ability in our uproarious abode. You can't buy that.

So when the car collapses, the lawnmower disintegrates, the tube freaks, and the stereo spits fire, we still have each other and able bodies. And who needs that extra dollar in the account anyway?

I RESIGN

Lord, I resign! I quit today! I left it all undone so my dear sweet husband would know what I do all day long besides wipe drippy faucets and referee brawls. Let this household find another Betty Crocker, Joan of Arc, and Phyllis Diller all rolled into one package! I've uttered "I'm not your servant" for the last time.

I've sincerely prayed, " 'Lord, make me an instrument of thy peace,' not a victim of it." What am I raising? A family or a grievance committee? Like Adam of old, I cry out, "Lord, you gave me all these menfolks and one tornadic daughter, so it's really your fault I'm unhinged!"

I never knew what 70 times 7 meant until I peered into the

bathroom and in my most lady-like fashion bellowed, "Who left those sopping towels on the floor again?"

Yes, I know; I stood before my father and that cloud of witnesses and promised in sickness and in health, poverty or wealth, for better or for worse. It's not the sickness and health nor the poverty or wealth. It's that sneaky "for better or for worse" that does us in every time! My father reminded us we were an omnibus in which the genes of our ancestors rode and the bus gets a bit shaky at times. Well, these ancestral genes are really vibrating and the old bus is tottering!

Why can't this able-bodied 6-foot, 3-inch man to whom I'm married rise and shine under his own steam? Must he back into every day?

And these bottomless pits I'm saddled with. When I remind them of their responsibilities, I'm a nagging shrew. "Mother, don't you think I've got enough sense to remember?" When I don't, it's still my fault! "Motherrrr, how could you let me forget?" What am I? Some mental trapeze artist, a glorified computer? Lord, you haven't forgotten I flunked freshman math!

And while I'm at it, how come I always have to be the one who says, "I'm sorry, I was wrong"? Couldn't those magic words be a part of my husband's vocabulary occasionally? How can he expect his offsprings to learn the meaning of those life-saver words if good ole Mom is the only one who 'fesses up?

Where can I go, Lord? The gypsies broke camp when the full moon waned. My mama told us we couldn't come running back home once we flew the coop. They've shut down the Foreign Legion. It was probably overrun with fugitives from motherhood suffering from omnibus tremors!

Wait a minute . . . I seem to remember. You've faced the problem of a disgruntled innkeeper before. "Martha, Martha, you are troubled over so many things." I have a sneaking suspicion there was more to the story of those two sisters than was recorded. I think I know what killed off Lazarus! Dear Martha. I bet she baked her bread and cakes from scratch, and Dr. Luke might well have stored his surgical instruments in her garbage jar without fear of contamination. But Mary—she was my daughter's kind of woman! She would have reveled in TV dinners and instant oatmeal. I can see her now—sitting placidly with a scroll amidst all that clutter, never dreaming of disturbing the ecology of her environment. She most likely outlived Martha by twenty years—at least.

How wise, how gentle you were with those sisters. With a touch of humor you weighed gastromical delights against eternity's values.

I'm tearing up my 126th resignation of the year. Help me learn to accept the minor aggravations of this omnibus. Don't let me whimper over nonessentials, making us all all miserable. Let me leap over these "for better or for worse" barriers!

Thank you for helping me recollect my tranquility. And now I shall consume my own smoke with an extra draught of hard work. "It is better to live in a corner of an attic than in a beautiful home with a crabby, quarrelsome wife."

BLESSINGS IN DISGUISE

"Wouldn't it be wonderful to meet a blessing that wasn't in disguise?"

"Mother, don't you wish you could just take off your backbone and hang it on a nail at night?"

"Don't worry about a thing! The medicine men have arrived. We'll massage your back every night. Have no fear, we are here! We'll take care of you." And so they did—one way or the other!

Here it was the first day of a brand new year, our wedding

anniversary; and I was unable to move without excruciating pain. Throb after throb of torture stalked up and down my spine and unwiped tears coursed down my cheeks. I wanted to shout against the wind! "Why? Why me, God? I have all these children and I can't move! They're school age now and can't go to their grandmothers'. It isn't fair! Why, Why?"

When the last why had died on my lips, merciful darkness and sleep came. Somewhere from that deeply submerged subconscious reservoir came the Shepherd's Psalm, so softly at first, I almost missed it. Then the phrase, "He *maketh* me to lie down" hovered over me ever so gently, yet persistently. He maketh me to lie down? Maketh? Then interruptions must have a place in your plans, and darkness, too. Continuous sun would torture us. In soul-stillness I surrendered my backbone to the Great Physician.

"I don't understand this, Lord, but someday I'll be in the presence of the One who can tell me why. I do know that you can mend broken bones and perform spiritual surgery on broken hearts. You can bring good out of any circumstance if we are willing to trust you to see us through. I give you my broken bones and heart, and when I come into your presence I don't think I'll need to ask why."

And then it was that God's Holy Spirit made intercession for me in ways too marvelous to comprehend. His grace is sufficient for any thorn of the flesh.

RICH IN EVERYTHING BUT MONEY

The only other female in our household was babbling away about the luxuries of one of her little friends. "Mother, she has three bathrooms, a swimming pool, and a four-poster bed and two dogs!" In the middle of all her bubbling and wishing,

Diane just stopped and gave me the sweetest smile. "Mother, I guess you could say we were rich in everything but money, couldn't you?"

It's true. Money is perhaps the commodity we have the least. We married back in the days when a car, a bank account, or the down payment on a house weren't considered absolutely essential for success. We had none of these.

Actually, two children graced our abode before we owned our first chariot. Our first TV came long after four offspring. We read together, worked in the yard, and swung and sang off-key in our old-fashioned swing.

Years and years later, our first "color TV" was a handmade grandfather clock. The second "color TV" was a used baby grand. "Do you think the third or fourth color TV could really be one?" the children sigh wistfully.

"We can't afford it" is a well-used phrase in our family vocabulary. Furthermore we use these words with no apology and no trace of feeling deprived. The art of doing without, and it is an art, has never warped or upset our children's psyches. The joy of saving, doing without, and waiting for our check, then delivery day! Twenty-three little people on our block treked through to see and hear grandfather chime.

Even more important, our children have grasped from us that neither money, large gifts, nor "things" can replace togetherness, family sharing, and anticipation of an event long-in-coming. Is not true prosperity the ability to enjoy what God has given us—whether little or much?

ONE WAY TO LEAVE THE HOSPITAL

My husband is such a marvelous, unpredictable necessity to me. For many years he's been a tower of strength on which to lean when our walls began to crumble under the combined weight of our overactive offspring. On numerous occasions he pats my shoulder, dries my tears, and tells me all four children take after my side of the house as he expresses sheer amazement that a mere mortal could have possibly fathered such a brood!

But there are times when he just folds up like a flower in the desert air. Take the day he fell from the hospital window, for instance. Shortly before noon our five-year-old Mark was performing his monkey act (not that he needed practice) atop the bars at the private school where we taught. In a moment of carelessness he slipped and fell to the asphalt beneath, splitting his chin. My husband, who taught Latin and glee club at the school, was summoned from class since the principal did not want to upset me and render me unable to continue my English classes.

Father and son set out for the emergency room of Baptist Hospital where the usual antiseptic odors vie for first place in the olfactory race. For some unknown reason my husband was perched in the window of the emergency room when the repair work on his namesake began. Upon seeing his own flesh and blood being sewed up, he toppled out of the window in a dead faint, badly bruising a shoulder and gashing an ear!

Meanwhile, school had dismissed for the day and I was searching for my family when someone told me one of the children had been hurt. The principal told me he'd sent father and son to the hospital some three hours before.

"Oh, no!" I cried. "You've made a terrible mistake! You sent the wrong parent to the hospital! I always clean up the blood, the diarrhea, the upchucking!"

In confirmation, the far hall door opened and in skipped son, smiling all over his neatly bandaged chin. Behind him limped Father, shoulders sagging and ear all bandaged. The principal, a husky football player who'd known my husband since college days, took one look at him and then asked a

49

question no wife in her right mind would have ever dared breathe.

In retrospect, my mind darted back to the July day this son was born. I had been cautioned to check in the hospital at the very first pang because of a broken back I had sustained. I made the error of announcing such news to my husband early that morning and suggesting I ride around Memphis with him to pick up the car pool.

"Car pool? What car pool? Oh, my goodness, I'll have to phone the fellers to get there the best way they can!"

Before I could even remember which bed I'd hidden the suitcase under, much less crawl under and get it, he rushed in, highly agitated. "The car won't start. Bet the battery's dead! We'll have to push it off the hill." Now there's one sure way to speed up delivery!

Before calling in the neighbors, I went out in the early morning air to survey the situation. I reminded him gently that for some unknown reason Bluebird had never started without one or the other of us turning on the ignition.

When son finally decided to appear at 10:15 that night, Father was fast asleep in the doctor's quarters. Ralph Bethea said he's never lost a father yet but that one was too close for comfort!

As I said, my Rock of Gibraltar is quite steady in life's ordinary crises when we have only 79 cents in the checking account or a student threatens my life. It's just these little circumstances where family blood is concerned that get him down!

GOOD MORNING, GOD

"Good morning, God. How are you doing today? Boy, I

bet you're tired after watching over the world all night long. Do you ever go to sleep?

I don't need a thing today. I'm doing fine. I just wanted to tell you hello and thank you for lots of things. And I wanted to know how you were getting along. You take care of so many people; how do you keep up with all of them without getting mixed up? But you don't have anybody to take care of you.

And that's why I'm not saying a "gimme prayer" today. Just a "thank you lots and how are you doing?" one today.

How are we to receive him? Like little children who go in and out of their father's house with joy. They are truly free! They really live by faith relinquishing cares, for they trust their father to provide all that is needed.

Children receive life unquestioningly as they come to it— moment by moment, day by day. They relish the "right now," finding beauty, wonderment, and magic everywhere. Feverish activities and worry about tomorrow are for grown-ups only!

Is it any wonder the Master said, "Whoever does not receive the kingdom of God like a child shall not enter it" (Mark 10:15)?

NOW I UNDERSTAND

Tears of gratitude blinded me as I made my way across the sleepy city to a hospital room one chilly Easter morn. As the blackness of the night surrendered to the dazzling kaleidoscope of dawn, thoughts of that first Easter engulfed me.

The women. Heartbroken. Making their way across a sleeping city in darkness. Carrying fragrances. Discussing how they could ever roll away so huge a stone. The swoop of dawn. A stone rolled away! Their burden lifted! Unspeakable joy! Swift footsteps to the city! He is alive! He is alive! Alive!"

I bowed my head. Women believe with their hearts, not their heads! My burden, like theirs, had rolled away! My son was alive! Alive!

He was so small to be in a coma—so very still. Why had I ever complained about his undiluted energy? Four days before David and Mark, after an overnight storm, ran up a split-level hill and climbed onto the edge of the dilapidated garage. Often they sat there, dangling their feet; never had they ventured beyond the edge.

We will never know what happened. Shortly before 9 A.M. Mark exploded through the kitchen door. "Mudder, hurry, hurry! David falled off the garage. He's just lying there and he won't speech to me!" The sight of that still, little form— on the concrete near the car—is etched forever in my memory. He had fallen headwise thirteen feet, barely missing the car.

It was an eternity of aloneness while the highway patrol located my husband in another state and escorted him homeward. An eternity for him, too, as they told him a family member was near death—nothing more.

After a spinal tap, the surgeon's brutal frankness. "Mrs. Thrash, I do not believe your son will ever come out of the coma. And if he does, there have been so many blood vessels burst in the brain, so much swelling, that in all probability, he will be hopelessly brain-damaged for life!"

An hour later my otherness found me sitting by the bed of our three-year-old deep in a coma. There was no change at dusk when my husband left to direct the music of a revival. Friends told me he sang "Let Not Your Heart Be Troubled" flawlessly. My faith was not so great.

"O God, let him live! Let him live! He was so banged up when he came into this world; one of his little feet was turned the wrong way. We've only had him three years, and we just can't do without this little feller! He was our bonus."

"Heavenly Father, I ask, I beg you to let him live, but don't let him be brain-damaged. What kind of life would that be? Please let him live, don't let that be his lot. Take him back to your home before that happens. Let him live and be whole! Please, dear God, please."

"You gave us David, and I'm ready for you to take over. I give him back to you. We've loved and enjoyed him so much; he rounded out that uneven three, and I don't know how we can do without him or how we'll manage his care if he's less than whole. But you'll teach us as you have done so often. I bow before your will, claiming your strength and heart peace. I've used all mine. I'm going home to our other children and leaving David with you."

At 9:30 that night David opened his eyes! He was not allowed to move from the shoulders up. One or the other of us remained beside him at all times. How do you keep a three-year-old still? When you know his very life depends upon total stillness, you find a way! Eternity crept by in these crucial hours and days.

"If David lives through Easter Sunday without hemorrhaging again, he has a good chance of making it," echoed over and over in my brain.

It was 6 A.M. Easter morn and David was alive! Dawn! The stone of time rolled away! Heartbreak transformed into unspeakable joy! He is alive. ALIVE!

Through tears I whispered, "Now I understand! O Father, for the very first time I understand!"

WHEN CAN I BE A TEENAGER?

Tiptoeing to the brink of adolescence, impatient with being a mere child saddled with unending house rules, Diane was most anxious to grow up. For two whole days she looked with disdain at her two younger brothers when they peered from under the branches of the oak tree and shrieked for her to join Tarzan and Cheeta.

"Daddy, I lay awake all night for a whole hour thinking about growing up and I want it to hurry. When do you think I can become a teenager?"

"Just as long as I can put it off, honey, just as long as I can put it off! Your brother is 12 years, 473 days old; I'm just not up to having a teenage son yet, much less a teenage daughter!"

One summer evening in the church parking lot a friend asked our youngest, "How old are you?" "Well, I've been four a mighty long time and I've gone to school a whole year and haven't even made it to the first grade yet!" David groaned.

Impatient with circumstances, I, like my children, want to get on with this business of living. Foolishly I try to chart an accelerated course by rushing things, people, events. "Hurryitis" twitches at my loose ends! Disappointment and disillusionment are always the outcome of such foolishness. A thousand years is but a day to him. Why fret and fume with impatience?

"Have you not known, have you not heard? The Lord is the everlasting God . . . . He does not faint or grow weary, his understanding is unsearchable . . . . They who wait on the Lord shall renew their strength, they shall mount up with wings like the eagles, they shall run and not be weary, they shall walk and not faint" (Isa. 40:28-31).

God never loses control of his purposes. The Holy Spirit works things together when the time is right! "Though it tarry, wait for it; because it will surely come" (Hab. 2:3, KJV).

We mortals live forward and understand backward. And it is difficult to get the forever straight.

I bring my "hurryitis" and anxiety to you, Master. Help it to grow up!

AREN'T MEMORIES WONDERFUL?

Who can ever forget the magic of a kindergarten graduation? A white picket fence strewn with exotic tissue flowers, one delirious director, painfully impatient dads, anxious moms, doting grandparents, squirming siblings waving and calling out, "Hi!" to older brother or sister while flashbulbs record the pandemonium for posterity.

After an unforgettable performance of mortar board topplers, a wise old six-year-old turned to her mother and sighed breathlessly, "Just think! This time last year I was graduating. Oh, Mother! Isn't it wonderful to have memories?"

Yes, oh, yes! So many memories line the pockets of my soul. A gallant stranger in a heavy transport truck paving the way, guiding, waiting if necessary for this young mother traveling alone with four wiggle worms over 150 miles of mountains and valleys, then giving a triumphant five-horn salute as we turned homeward from the highway.

Which of us can forget that odd noise interrupting thoughts of a quiet congregation witnessing the baptism of our eldest? Then the hushed voice of David echoing to the rafter, "*That's Doug* scraping his feet on the bathtub!"

Mark good-naturedly grouching, "Mother, how can I ever get to be a bachelor? You're turning me into an old maid with all this woman's work!"

David who dreams in living color, asking shyly, "Mother, when you say 'Just a minute,' will that be a woman's minute?"

Diane, curled up under the table reading poetry to a fat, pumpkin-colored cat. "Cinnamon can do math, too. Just watch him thump his tail nine times when I ask him to add 5 plus 4! He doesn't understand this new math; he likes the old stuff."

The disarming honesty of a wide-eyed Doug. "Boy, the

Fords said their conscience had been hurting them because they hadn't had us over to eat or taken us out. Well, I got a load of that bill at the restaurant tonight—$59.63. Brotheeerr! I bet their conscience doesn't hurt them again for a long time!"

Children's young years are something to be preserved forever in a mason jar. So swiftly they slip by! As Granny Thrash says, "Children tug at your apron strings when they're small and your heart strings as they grow up!" But we can't cling to our young. Grow and go they must! And we must grow, too. After all, being young is a fault which improves daily.

Part 11
My Larger Family

And who is my neighbor?

WORLD, HERE I COME

Being born in the Carson-Newman College gymnasium—my older brother and I were the only species born in captivity—was prophetic of my galloping gait in life! During those young years of wedded life I rushed around my domain attending the usual diapers, dirty dishes, and dusting marathon. After nap time in the afternoon ("Mother, why is it every time you get tired we take a nap?"), I operated the only homemade cookie dispensing machine in the whole neighborhood in between baseball camp and bicycle riding lessons. Why, I had more Purple Hearts from being wounded by a bicycle than all the other mothers put together. Indeed, my stamina was so great, I could have brought honor to my country in almost any event of the Olympics.

During my decade of mothering from one to four preschoolers, I realized they must not become too dependent on me or I on them. Smother-love is deadly! Joyously I fulfilled my role of wife and mother, but deep inside me I nurtured and fanned that faint but stubborn spark of creativity that belonged to me alone. I was "Willard's Otherness," but often I asked, "Who else am I?" I read everything I could get my hands on and jotted down insights and observations in my "Someday Notebook."

As I conversed with my pots and pans each evening, hoping to retain my fleeting sanity, I reminded myself of all the feats I'd accomplished. My list was endless. How I longed to sit at my sewing machine and whip up a number that could be safely worn on some occasion other than Halloween! For years I'd done the family mending while the children took turns removing the bobbin, running the needle through each other's fingers while I dashed off to rescue a boiling pot.

I'd spent many wistful moments gazing at those colorful homemade rugs. I was determined to hook one of those before joining the senile set. In exchange for my long years of faithful service, my family surely would allow me to put my finished creation in the carport to catch the oversupply of oil our gas-guzzling hearse spewed forth!

Oh, yes! There was that dresser drawer overflowing with illegible, moth-eaten manuscripts. But my heart really soared when I noted the oldest senior at Sarah Lawrence was fifty-four. By jove, if she could, what was I waiting for?

Need I tell you my rug is still unhooked, my fashions uncreated, and most of my manuscripts unheralded? But I have emerged from my slightly battered cocoon, dusted the cobwebs of time from my brain, and traded my kitchen for a classroom.

How? To the brave prepared to launch out into the deep—for it is an exercise in faith—I have only three exhortations.

1. Plot your priority and let it take precedence over all else. Murder the alternatives, or you'll always be looking back. "This one thing I do . . . " not these forty things I dabble in.

2. Be kind to yourself. Enlist and involve the family in your goal. Don't do things they can do for you or for themselves. Use all available shortcuts. Toss out excess baggage and trivialities.

3. Remember. Self-development takes discipline, dedica-

tion. Never mind what others think. Ignore others' expectations of you. Forego impossible standards maintained for the sole approval of friends, neighbors, or relatives. This only saps your energy and fragments your mind. In short, "To thine own self be true . . ." with not a tinge of guilt or self-reproach.

Results? Unbelievable! Sheer exhilaration of matching wits with a much younger generation. Realization that time has not deteriorated your billions of brain cells. Intuitive flashes and insights that come with maturity alone. That "born again" feeling of inner joy and exuberance children experience can be yours in the process of relearning, reorganizing, and refining that which you already have. The best cosmetic in the whole world is an active mind discovering something new and putting wings to that discovery.

MOTHER'S OVER THE HILL—TO GRAD SCHOOL

Help! Mother's traded in the kitchen stove on a classroom! Do they send CARE packages to American boys? I bet Daddy can collect from Medicare after his very first bite.

Such was our three sons' somewhat less-than-enthusiastic reception of the news that twelve-year-old sister would prepare lunch each day while one mother of ancient vintage tottered home from the halls of learning. According to the boys, anyone thirty-five or more was a real relic who had lived in the "olden" days.

All the family shared in the Mainstreaming Mama Project; a weekly list was posted with rotating goodies. There were good-natured gripes about soggy sandwiches, malnutrition, and the possibility of rickets. Things ran rather smoothly until Daddy got carried away in the marketplace and invited guests with the usual fifteen-minute notice. Daughter became so unglued she mixed the grape Kool-Aid with a pitcher of iced tea. Mark and David drank it anyway, declaring it made good cough syrup for summer colds. Doug allowed if we ever found ourselves in desperate financial straits, we could bottle it for medicinal purposes. What with bracing two sets of teeth and buying a new home, I figured we might be peddling that potion a lot sooner than he thought.

As for me, I felt a strange kinship to that goodly woman, of whom I'd always been a bit suspicious, in the thirty-first chapter of Proverbs. (To be downright honest, I'd planned to have a few choice words with her in the hereafter since she'd ruined Mother's Day for me.) Suddenly I found myself rising while it was yet night, not to provide food for my household as much as to study Strauss Syndrome or statistics. It seemed my lamp never went out. Willard declared I studied in my sleep. I had no time to eat the bread of idleness although I longed to sink into Polynesian paralysis. My husband was known in the city gates and I had a sneaking suspicion he would have preferred to stay there rather than come home to a preoccupied wife. One evening I set all my special education notes on fire while cooking and studying for a final. Doug decided we'd best invest in fire-fighting equipment or soda in the five-pound boxes.

Each afternoon as I slid into home plate, eight kids of assorted sizes awaited me to take them swimming. Promptly at 3:30 I would remind them the lifeguard had to go home, type up her notes, study, and cook. Never was there any arguing or protest; all were so proud to have a genuine relic who could still lifeguard and get educated too!

On report card day all four offspring were sitting on the front steps. "We'll have to see the grades before Mother can go swimming today," they informed the other four. We went as scheduled.

A demanding summer? You bet! It demanded patience

and a great sense of humor on the part of my lively family. Of me, it demanded self-confidence, commitment, constancy, and the ability to laugh to and at myself.

But the exciting renaissance, the *elan vital* is worth every sacrifice of honoring your dreams, on which there is no ceiling!

HANK IS HUMAN!

Hank shuffled into my heart on a broiling September day. Dirty blonde hair that resembled a droopy sheep dog, slanting eyes blue with defiance, stumbling gait—these were his trademarks.

Suspended from two schools and declared impossible in the third, Hank had been placed in special education. And I, a mere mortal setting up the first program in the city, inherited the task of making him manageable.

Hank lived up to his usual reputation the first few weeks. Our classroom was an airless alcove off the stage which put Hank in kicking and punching distance of every boy, and he took full advantage of the situation. According to him, all mischief originated with the other guys; never was he at fault. They all picked on him.

Hank balked, he sulked, he threw tantrums, he fought everybody. In desperation one afternoon I pored over every scrap of his record, the fattest in the file. Neurological damage, brain injury, hand-eye coordination quite difficult . . . had many pairs of glasses bought for him but too stubborn to wear them . . . malformed hip socket. Father, under influence of alcohol, often beat him because Hank was so different from others. If Hank broke anything, he ran away to escape punishment.

Mother beyond coping with the situation while trying to work. I closed the file and sat for a long time wondering if he had ever had a chance in life.

At the end of three weeks I, too, was ready to throw up my hands and declare him a misfit! Didn't he realize in my class I had six other boys with problems? He was a terror at home, tyrannizing his sisters, refusing to pick up anything, causing a tidal wave in the bathroom every time he was forced to take a bath, staying out on the streets until midnight or after, and on and on.

After three continuous periods of Hank, I was ready for the resuscitation squad, and the year had barely begun! But I was just as pig-headed as he. After all, he was in my program for nine months, and one of us was going to have to get along with the other, and I jolly well knew which one it would be.

There is no formula for success in special education. You've had a successful day if you have enough energy to drive the car home. Hank gave up without a try all that first month; then I noted a small dent in his armor. All the boys brought news clippings which we read and discussed. Hank breathed drag racing, so I was all prepared for such a clipping. Instead, he brought a nutshell editorial from a country philosopher. It was a simple story about a man who had planted a tree when his first son was born. Both son and tree grew to maturity. When the son strayed out of line, the father corrected him in love. The father also pruned and straightened the tree if it bent too much to one side. The philosopher concluded that both son and tree grew tall in the world because of a wise father. Blinking away tears, I read it to the whole class as he requested. In his fumbling way, Hank told me he'd like that kind of dad. Unbidden from my memory bank came these words, "It takes only the sunshine and rain of love to make the bent plant straighten."

Hank's academic achievements were few and far between. Scolding, lecturing, or shaming him were to no avail; he'd had a lifetime of scorn. I usually announced to my boys that Hank wasn't even going to try today, and he would—just to make a liar out of me! He could add, but subtraction was a foreign language, so we added like crazy and forgot subtraction. Another guy who liked to subtract did that. Reading or phonics were alien areas. Anything mechanical fascinated him.

"Mrs. Tflash (as he called me), don't they teach you how to load a stapler in college? You're so dumb!"

Hank set up and ran the projector, and I risked civil war if I dared let anyone within plugging distance of that projector. I've seen him mumble, stomp, and reach the boiling point; but he never gave up on that machine.

Shortly after Thanksgiving, Hank went on one long tantrum. Only an angel could have wrestled with him, and I was far from an angelic state. The shop teacher stopped by my alcove one afternoon.

"Mrs. Thrash, do you know Hank's dad bolted Saturday night? After a loud scene he walked out on them. No money, no food except a jar of peanut butter and jelly."

The shop teacher often took Hank home and had been called into the house by Hank's mother. "I've arranged to buy Hank's lunch each day in exchange for sweeping out the shop. I'm working on other help. Would you do the same?"

Pieces of the puzzle began to fall in place. I went off alone and just put myself into that frail, shuffling body and peered at a hostile world through those sunken eyes. If I'd had little or no food for three days and had seen my world, such as it was, dashed to pieces, would I have reacted any differently? Hank's dad never returned.

The day before Christmas holidays began, I gave my students a big party at our home. Hank insisted that he would bake a cake for the occasion despite protests that it would poison us all. Came party day, and in shuffled Hank with the cake no one expected to see; he had the cafeteria ladies guard it until party time. We walked the few blocks to my house with Hank grumbling about his tired feet the whole way. He carried the cake one block and I the next. I knew his mother had baked it since it had toothpicks to keep the icing from sliding, but I bragged over and over about his masterpiece. He insisted the first piece was to be my husband's. Hank blossomed that morning as he touched every Christmas ornament in the entire house, sat under our eight-foot tree flicking the lights on and off, gobbled food, and accepted compliments on his cake. The only complaint came from a buddy who ate the toothpicks.

Winter surrendered to spring and I marveled that both Hank and I had survived. Under all those layers of indifference he knew I really cared for him; therefore I could not give in to his tantrums. I set limits and boundaries—generous ones which he understood—and expected him to operate within this framework. When he exceeded his limits, I disciplined him firmly and fairly with no outward show of emotion. If he refused to sweep, he didn't eat ice cream in the cafeteria. Other deprivations involved his drag racing and hot rod books. This consistency was new to him, since he'd been beaten by his father, indulged by a bewildered mother, and ignored by his siblings. In frequent conferences with his mother, I explained I accepted Hank where he was, not where I'd like him to be, and worked from there. This was much easier for me since I was not emotionally involved as a mother usually is.

One morning I struggled to school so shaky from a twenty-four-hour virus I could hardly lift my head. My class took care of me. Hank brushed my forehead.

"You're sick! You better git on home! Take a day or two off." Then Hank shuffled around the room. "Pipe down,

George! Can't you see Mrs. Tflash is sick? Danny, knock it off, you goon! Ain't you got no manners?" Hank made more noise than all the class put together, but his concern for me was genuine.

School wore on, and my patience wore out—many times. Hank refused to do his share of getting the cafeteria ready for lunch. He'd much rather fight, tease, or sneak to the kitchen for a handout. The custodian who trained my boys restrained himself from cracking Hank on the head with a broom. My vocational counselor declared Hank would be in a home for wayward boys and I at a rest farm for demented teachers before June.

When we came to the section on auto repairs, Hank perked up. If I stumbled over a word, he corrected me with his usual "tact." He assured me of my complete stupidity in between poring over all the catalogs on auto parts and racing.

Our final outing—a train ride to a nearby city and a picnic on the beach—found Hank sitting by me. He grumbled because the train was doing only 80 MPH. "You know, I walked three miles to your house Saturday. Saw you playing Ping-Pong with your boys, but I chickened out and din't ring the door bell."

I smiled to myself. "Now that's all I need to push me over the brink. Hank on a Saturday!" That final day, of which I'd deliriously dreamed, rolled around, and after the assembly award program, I sat and talked with my boys.

"Fellows, I won't be back with you next year. My boss has given me a big honor. I'm going to another school that's never had a program and get it going for them. You're going to have a big army man who used to be a colonel. He can run lots faster, pitch better, and he doesn't have a busted back so he can help you weed your garden . . . ."

"That does it! I don't want no army man. I'm not comin' back to this crummy school next year and nobody can make me!"

The boys grinned at me knowingly; it took us all to manage Hank.

"Don't let him bug you, Mrs. Thrash. Remember, Big Mouth used to blow his stack every Friday and tell us he wasn't coming back on Monday; but he always showed up. You know, he tries to come on big, but Hank's human, after all!"

My year's experience with Hank and his mother holds no price tag. I saw a bent, wilted plant slowly straighten and grow tall.

BLESS THIS ROAST

As dear friend Carolyn Rhea used to say in seminary days, "This is my missionary roast!" We shared it with a new family in our church today. How they enjoyed that brown gravy made from the drippings. But far more important than the roast was the hunger of our newfound friends, high up in management circles, for fellowship, friendship, and acceptance. They drank in every object de art in our modest surroundings. The daddy brought us a watermelon, and their lads heaved watermelon rinds with every bit as much gusto as ours in a sneaky, after-dark battle!

Where did we get the mistaken assumption that people with position were to be envied because they had everything?

Another new family—so young as to have three wee ones, so plagued with financial and employment problems—shared a larger roast. The little ones had had only cereal and peanut butter sandwiches that day. They actually needed more food than fellowship. As I cleared away the last crumb, I felt we'd entertained angels unaware. How You multiplied our roast, just as You multiplied the loaves and fishes long ago on a hillside! They gathered the leftovers, too.

I can't scale the mountain or cross stormy seas to minister to others; my kitchen is so often my mission field. But is not evangelism one beggar telling another where to find bread? And is a distant shore more favored than your own neighborhood?

Oh, I know I've griped about being Mrs. Zacchaeus when two extras turn up and there are no spares in sight. The day my honey, unknowingly, brought the district manager home to scrape the turkey bones—"Best turkey stew I ever put in my mouth!"—was such a shock that he refrained from bringing anyone home for ten whole days.

Life is so daily! Master, don't ever let me get so busy, so preoccupied with self and family that I miss out on the blessing of sharing. Continue to bless and multiply our roast, ham, spaghetti, peanut butter cookies, or whatever you've given us.

OUR MARTHA

Martha interrupted our complacent lives early one winter evening. Answering a gentle rap at our door, I came face to face with Martha, who was standing in softly falling rain. Born of well-to-do parents in Spain, educated in Cuba, she was now a displaced person in the city of Miami.

"Please, Mrs. Thrash, I hear you help people with English. My Mama, she knows not it, and she is so lonesome. I want better to learn your beautiful language, too. Will you help the both of us?"

My caller had come in out of the rain, and we discussed the two nights available for English lessons. On impulse, I took a church bulletin from my desk and explained it to my newfound friend.

"Martha, you've told me how lonely you and your mother are. I'd like for both of you to come to worship with us this Sunday. Your mother wouldn't understand too much, but she'd enjoy the music and feel the warmth of the people. We have a cure for loneliness. Will you come?

Sunday dawned cool and cloudy. Attendance was off; my faith was small. I prayed a silent prayer. Near the end of opening assembly, Martha and her mother slipped in. I greeted them warmly, practicing my limited Spanish with Mama. She understood little of the lesson or worship service, but she closed her eyes and clasped her hands during my husband's solo. Every few minutes she would smile, reach over, and pat one of our younger sons on the head.

On the night of our first lesson, we delayed our family altar until our new friends came. They joined the circle, and Mama Rodriguez's eyes danced as we sang "Only Believe" slightly off key. She had a simple lesson in household objects, and Martha had a more advanced one. I asked if we might read Psalm 23!

"What does it mean—a staff? How does God prepare a table in front of his enemies? Can you not be afraid of death?"

All my life I'd known this beautiful psalm. Yet I learned something new from seeking minds that night.

Martha came to her next lesson alone because Mama was ill. We read Psalm 103 at the close of our lesson, and I marked some of my favorite passages in the new Spanish-English Bible my husband had brought us.

"I have lost my job as my license has—how do you say it?—run out and I have no money for lessons. But I want so much not to give them up."

I assured her she was to continue for lack of money didn't concern me. Then we prayed about her job, and I gave her a chocolate cake I'd baked for Mama.

On the following Saturday Martha was going to our church picnic with us. Before breakfast she was on our doorstep.

"I have a new job; I can no go to picnic, but I give you potato salad to take for me."

Our friendship deepened. The family physician had said Mama was unable to continue so Martha drove across the city alone. English idioms were Martha's downfall and delight. "How you say that again?" She called if she was unable to attend lessons or church. We always ended our study with the English-Spanish Bible.

One Sunday afternoon Martha called and asked to come over and read the Bible with me. Asking the Holy Spirit to be my helper, I presented the plan of God's love in simplicity. We read passages from her Bible, both in Spanish and English.

"Oh, how I wish this joy of Jesus in my heart, also! But I cannot forgive the man who caused Mama's brother's death!"

Words tumbled out, followed by weeping. Her mother's brother had planned a daring escape shortly after midnight on a certain night. He told only a trusted family friend. Two hours before his escape, police came to the home and shot him. Since that terror-filled night, Mama's mind had never been the same, and physicians gave her no hope of recovery.

"Martha, oh, Martha, now you know how God felt when his only Son was betrayed and killed by an angry, bloodthirsty mob. He was heartbroken. That was his Son! You can't handle your hate. Only God is able to do that. Only he is wise enough to know what to do with it. Martha, do you remember the night we read Psalm 37? [Don't get upset about the wicked.] . . . For they will soon fade like grass, and wither like a green [plant]. Trust in the Lord.

"Martha, God alone is able to bring something good out of this terrible deed—the same way he brought good from his Son's murder. He can't forgive you unless you are willing to turn your hate over to him. You can't get rid of it, but he can do it for you. Martha, you can't come to Jesus on your terms. Only on his!"

No longer able to speak, I put my arms around Martha, and we wept together. In a few minutes her sobbing quietened. She dried those tears and with a radiant smile announced her readiness to give her heart to Jesus on his terms. Joy bells in heaven sounded!

I took her to our pastor's study, where she spoke to him briefly. "A big burden has just been lifted right from my heart!" She was the first to respond to the invitation and with trembling rejoicing, I translated her testimony. There were no dry eyes that night as she said it had not been easy for her to hand over her hate to God.

An entire church celebrated her birthday with her some weeks later. Martha is no longer within driving distance of our church. Her mother's condition is quite serious; many times she doesn't recognize Martha. Her new faith has been severely tested. "Pray for me every day. I must stay with Mama. Life is hard, and when I am not able to come to church, my joy goes dim."

Thank you, Martha, for interrupting our lives that winter evening. Thank you for teaching our children that Christian compassion knows no race, language, or color barrier.

YOU BELIEVED IN ME!

"You are the best teacher I ever had! You believed in me. I ain't able to read or write or even print much on 'count of this learning block. But you found things I could do and told me I was good at them while everyone else always told me how dumb I was. I was the best air-conditioner fixer or meter fixer.

"I seen that funny look on yer face when I snuck that perfume and hankie on yer desk as a farewell present. Mrs. Thrash, I didn't heist that from Zayre's or anywhere like that!

I knowed you heard 'bout my swiping a car or two, even if you never said anything 'bout it. But honest to God, I paid for that, and my sister picked it out for you.

"Us guys are ready to come over there and get you back as our teacher. You never hollered even at ole Henry.

"If I ever hear anybody putting you down I'll knock them down. I hope your new class is good to you and you like wearing the perfume I bought for you."

Love,
Ken

My sister wrote this for me. Write.

Boynton Beach, Florida
December 12, 1967

ODE TO WILLARD ET UX, ET AL

It is hard to say how much we'll feel
   The void your leaving will bring.
Your Seven Part Harmony we feel
   In word, in song, and deed.

Each one seventh of your household strong
   Has made a niche with our clan—
In class, choir loft, at home, at play
   Attuned to God all the way.

Go forth, Willard et ux, et al,
   Bless others as you have blessed us.

George, Rosanne, Gail, and Alan

December 1, 1967
(Upon our departure from Boynton Beach, Fla.)

MY FRIEND DIED TODAY

Nancy died today. Only twenty-nine, she went too soon, but she was so very tired. Kidneys collapsed, frail shell shackled with raging infection, blinding pain. But it was loss of sight that finally crushed her spirit. Her heart ever so gently gave up. Thank you, God, for her release, for calling my dear friend home to your mansion. A bruised reed you will not break, smoking flax you will not quench. You knew *when*, Lord. It isn't my place to ask *why?*. In every need you are previous! Your grace is sufficient. Sufficient for Dick, for Rick, for little Cheryl. They have been so wonderfully brave, and I'm thanking you ahead for what you will do for them. And now I go to my memory box, and tears of release flow for dreams undone.

Dearest Friend,

Only wish I could express myself with pen and words. It would really take a book to list your acts of love during each of those numerous hospital trips. If you had done none of those I'd owe you a big heaping thanks just for being "Catey Thrash." You'll never know what being close to you has meant to me these past two years. What a living example you've been! I could never have made it without you. For there were days on end I just knew God had forgotten me, and I was ready to give up when along came "Catey" and she'd always find a patch of blue and remind me God does not forget us! Your advice, if you could call it that, was priceless, and I'd almost understand why? as I've asked that question so often. I'll always remember each shared moment and cherish it for whatever lifetime I have. Thank you for all you've done, but mostly for being just "Catey" and helping me be a better person.

                                                I love you,
                                                Nancy

Long distance for the third time today asking simply, "When will you get here?" They knew we were coming. And now we are beginning the journey on Your day. Keep our three here safe while we are gone. Help them to be kind to one another.

And, Lord, thank you again for Nancy. Even as she was dying she was reconciling! Just as you. A father and mother who had been too busy making a living to have any time for you. A rebellious church member who'd turned her back on you. Doctors, nurses in so many cities were amazed at her faith! A church revived! The cripple at the fruit stand where we used to go. And now we all give her back to you.

She'll be beautiful in her Christmas dress! "Catey, red's our favorite color, and I'm going to glory in bright red!

Give her something very special to do!

INVADING A SISTER COUNTRY

Canada may experience another centennial before she recovers from our month of houseswapping! This invasion of our sister country had its incubation period many months before the actual journey when a Canadian pastor invited my husband to preach in his pulpit and abide in his abode for a month. We, in turn, arranged a Florida vacation less than a mile from the ocean's edge for our Canadian friend, who had been a classmate of ours in graduate school. Both men kept the postal services of each country in business with an exchange of maps, travel folders, sightseeing tips, shopping hints, and instructions about various idiosyncrasies of each household.

At long last we bade farewell to the shores of Florida in

early July. Neighbors, peering cautiously at our overburdened, gas-guzzling hearse of ancient vintage, suspected we were fleeing the country for good. As we left the gates of the city in darkness, our radio played such a stirring rendition of the national anthem I felt I was departing for Russia! My better half grumbled about all the other assorted nuts on the highway at that ungodly hour. According to him, anyone who voluntarily greeted the dawn before 8 A.M. was a wee bit touched.

Dave, our youngest son, was all set to watch the day creep up on the night, but he fell asleep shortly before the production occurred. At 8 A.M. my husband began reminding himself to get up, even though he was driving by then. Breathing deeply, we left the palms of the south and drove to mid-state where lakes shimmered and orange trees glistened with dew.

"Do you think Canada is ready for US?" And, "Daddy, why couldn't we bring our portable dishwasher? We're taking everything else," queried middle son Mark.

By 9:30 Douglas was threatening to report us to the Society of Prevention of Cruelty to Children because he'd had no food for five whole hours. Usually he's inhaled three breakfasts by then!

Lunch was devoured under pine trees on the bank of the Suawanee River. Our enterprising descendants suggested we help finance the trip by dipping our plastic forks in the historic river and selling them as souvenirs in Ottawa.

We celebrated young David's tenth birthday on our second day en route. "Daddy, I was wadded up in this back seat going someplace on my last birthday! Do you think we will every be anyplace on my birthday?"

When our caravan groaned across the Kentucky line, the boys were quite disappointed that Colonel Sanders didn't spring forth with a big drumstick in each hand. At the end of our second day's journey, the lights of Cleveland, Ohio, loomed ahead. Suddenly we heard a frightful knock and felt a strong vibration. The culprit proved to be a broken universal joint. It was quite a jolt for our eldest, who suffers from acrophobia, to awaken at midnight, open the door, and discover he was twelve feet airborne on a hydraulic lift!

Repairs on the hearse were completed by 12:30 A.M. so we decided to continue to Buffalo and have a full day at the Falls. However, there was a slight seven-hour delay when my husband took the wrong turn on the turnpike and drove to Indiana instead! "Someone around here needs to enroll in an adult education course in map reading," issued forth from the back seat. By the time we arrived in Buffalo again, the children were pouring Scope on Doug's toes and spraying them with Right Guard.

Although this was my third visit to the Falls, I stood in silent awe. Massive, tumbling powerhouse of energy spouting angry spray!

"Only God could have created this," Diane marveled.

"Good grief! Who turned on that giant-sized faucet? Man, I'd hate to pay that water bill," blurted Mark.

Returning to the parking lot on the American side, we discovered a rear window of the wagon tailgate had fallen into a coma. We spent the next two hours in repair while our elated sons drooled over a dozen GTOs, racing cars, and a gold Model T. By evening Doug was accepting wagers on what part of the chariot would fall out next. "Flat tire in Chattanooga, radiator repair in Kentucky, universal joint in Ohio, window repair in Niagara. Shucks! We're replacing this heap piece by piece!"

When gently admonished about his questionable activity, he reminded us vacations were for doing something different, and accepting wagers sure was different!

Glory be! We entered the Promised Land at 4:01 on the fourth afternoon. One more day of being locked up with four offspring, and my demented husband would have hired out the whole lot as grape stompers in upstate New York! He believed in original sin, but after this he was convinced of the total depravity of the soul! As we passed through customs, a voice piped up from the third seat, "Quick, Mark, hide your marijuana cigars!"

Driving into the yard of our exchange home, we breathed a prayer of thanksgiving for delivering us from each other. Before Willard could even undo the groaning luggage carrier, Diane clomped out onto the porch in floppy wooden shoes, shaking cha cha sticks in either hand and yelling, "Welcome to Canada. Bon soir! Bon soir!"

"That daughter of yours is riding back in the luggage carrier!" growled her dad.

HOUSESWAPPING, CANADIAN STYLE

Ottawa, once a logging town, was something straight from Grimm's fairy lore. Each day netted a new discovery. A windmill only a few blocks from our home, the Rideau Canal winding its way through the city, gardens with neat rows of vegetables, and fruit trees sprinkled in every yard. Roses, snapdragons, and lilies spilling over rocks.

My bouts with Canadian cookery were something else! Finding a large can of Canadian *pur* on the drainboard, I took it to be shortening. Hurling a few dollops [blobs] into the electric skillet, I began my famous meatballs. Belatedly, I realized *pur* was honey after the skillet began to smoke and turn black. However, Willard pronounced those as the best sweet-sour meatballs of my entire Epicurean career.

Meat prices were all but prohibitive; fresh fruits and vegetables were even worse! Tomatoes were 69 cents a pound so we did without. Lettuce, a bargain at 15 cents, became daily fare until the boys said they were sprouting rabbit ears. Our clan kept the nearby bakery operating as we bought sixty-seven loaves of buttercrust, rye, wheat, French, potato, and pumpernickel bread. Our bread gal, Diane, would rush home with a warm loaf, which usually disappeared before the meal began. Bread dripping with *pur* replaced peanut butter as the filler-upper.

Parliament Hill, resplendent in medieval surroundings and soaring above the Ottawa River, was our favorite. We hastened there the first morning to see that ancient military ritual, the changing of the guard, and we recorded the sight and sound. Evening after evening we returned to the magic of the hill. The sky was ablaze with stars, a thousand lights twinkled in the bay, and a brilliantly lighted cross on a church steeple beckoned us from across the river. Strains of history and voices from the past greeted us at the "Sound and Light Production." Cheery tourists waved to us from the famed Chateau Laurier Castle as a gypsy moon played hide-and-seek, darting through buttermilk clouds.

The Centennial Flame, leaping from the fountain on Parliament Lawn, was a favorite gathering place. The boys were ready to extract their Expo spending money from its waters. Near the flame was the Queen's Box. We spied our politician at the podium one evening, "Now if you elect me as your first lady Prime Minister, I promise you: No increase in taxes and lollipops on the Parliament Lawn every night at eight!"

Of all the concerts—carillon bells, folk singers, bands, youth groups—the carillons in the Peace Tower were our favorite. Made of fifty-three bells, the largest 22,400 pounds and the smallest a mere ten, the instrument is played from a wooden keyboard after the Flemish system of centuries ago.

We adopted Ottawa, wandering through all the surrounding hills, valleys, and hamlets. An elderly park guard gave us fruit to sample, then chuckled with nostgalia as he watched all four undignified offspring roll down a steep hill and land unceremoniously on their posteriors.

In astonishment we viewed our first cricket match in living color on a Sunday afternoon. A short time later the *Nutcracker Suite* sprang to life as we watched a parade of soldiers march to their tiny guard boxes at the Governor General's Mansion.

Truly, this was Willard's city since only Americans rushed. Each day we sat in our neighbor's yard or on his back porch. Old and young alike lingered in small groups on Parliament Lawn long after the concert was finished. Clerks in gift shops exchanged pleasantries and inquired about my accent. "People actually take time to live!" was my husband's amazing observation.

We waited two weeks for an appointment to tour the mint. "Hey, Daddy, maybe they give away free samples! Do you think they'll let you take up a collection?"

Of course, no one in his right mind would miss Expo—or so we thought. On Mark's eleventh birthday we and 366,712 others went to the fair! After waiting in line two-and-a-half hours, we noted that wheelchair people were advanced in the impossible lines. Willard suggested renting one for me, with all of us taking a turn when nobody was looking. It took two weeks of recovery before we sampled Expo again.

On our last Sunday we were dinner guests of a nearby family. Our hostess carefully warmed the plates in the oven along with the roast, a custom I hadn't seen since early childhood days in East Tennessee. The meal was lovely and very formal. Even their smallest child had impeccable manners. As our host carved the roast and served the plates, Douglas nudged me and asked what in the world should he do with that tiny, round plate (individual bread plate). Had I been a complete failure in the manners department? Shortly before dessert, five-year-old Bonnie, the youngest,

80

carefully picked up her plate and licked the remaining brown gravy, exclaiming with gusto, "Mommie, that was delicious!" We all but hugged her in relief.

We could have remained in Ottawa until the first snowfall. Church bells breaking the silence on a sleepy Lord's Day morn, shy, warm welcomes by neighbors, the gallantry of the men, even the hippies—whom Willard conversed with daily. All unforgettable!

Sadly we bade adieu to our adopted city at 2 A.M. on the last day of July. "Quick, Mother, put her in reverse! We've got to go back. I've lost my gold-plated toothpick!"

In imagination we gave the gallant, sleeping city a twenty-one gun salute as a drowsy voice broke the silence.

"Mexico, prepare yourself! You're our next victim!"

A CUP OF COLD WATER

The Florida dawn, scattering its dazzling rays across the sky, awakened me. Before beginning my usual Saturday marathon, I prayed, "Father, if someone needs your help today—someone that we can help—send them to us or us to them." What strange pathways this daily prayer often led; how many interruptions to the day's plans it sometimes brought! Yet, I had no right to pray it unless I meant business with God.

The morning passed pleasantly with all the yard work. At noon we lingered around the table for our family altar, since we were eating with friends that night. The discussion centered around Jesus' ministering to people's needs and bringing out the best in them while the Pharisees only sought to criticize and find fault.

"We've been here only a week and have just one neighbor nearby, but we don't sit around feeling sorry for ourselves.

I'm sure God will send someone who needs our family," my husband told our somewhat lonesome brood.

Little did he know how true his statement would be! In less than two hours a speeding car overturned across the highway directly in front of our house. Then our front patio was filled with Mexican migrant workers. My fumbling Spanish deserted me in this emergency as we rushed to gather up blankets for those in shock, as well as call an ambulance, the police, and notify the fire department for the ancient car had exploded. Although a language barrier was present, we were able to convey our deep concern. Daughter ran around "Buenos Diasing" all of them.

After all the drama and excitement had subsided and the frame of the car had been towed away, David, not the least surprised, looked at his dad and remarked thoughtfully, "Well, it sure didn't take God very long to answer our prayer, Daddy!"

"And whoever gives to one of these little ones . . . a cup of cold water" (Matt 10:42). How many times we fail to give a cup of cold water because we are waiting for something really important to do for our Lord. So often priceless opportunities go begging because we try to lay down the terms or conditions of service instead of accepting that which he wisely sends us. God is God of the mundane as well as the big events. There is a down-to-earth quality about his care.

Late that night I knelt by my bed. "Thank you, oh, thank you for letting us be the Holy Spirit's vehicle today! We forget all about self. Thank you for making these little ones Mexican; we didn't ask that, but we're so glad they were. And, Jesus, thank you for faith's simplicity shown again by a child who knew his daddy's prayer would be answered! Don't let us live so fast, run so hard that we miss those in need. Do away with our blindness, our laziness! We can't, but you can."

EMPTY NEST VACCINE

"You are the recipient of a Master's Fellowship at the University of South Florida. If for any reason you cannot accept . . . ." Any reason I can't accept! I clutched the magic message and barreled down to the end of the road to await my husband. "Honey, guess what—guess what!"

That was fifteen months ago. Today I tottered across the finish line, picking up that degree in special education, realizing a three-year dream (or nightmare). I logged 14,000 miles on the I-4 Grand Prix. All summer long I've hurled out of the driveway before 7 A.M., attended three straight classes, then lay down and panted in the parking lot before completing my sixty-five-mile marathon for the day.

In addition to maintaining a near 4.0 average, I've managed our eight-room waterfront "motel," taught a Bible class each Sunday, and entertained the usual mobs. Project Educating Mama has been a liberal education for all of us, requiring great esprit de corp. Some of our misadventures include: David's telling the Friday vegetable man, "We just can't afford any; we're on an economy binge trying to get Mother through school!" Diane's wailing, "Daddy took one look at the meal and said he had to get back to the office!" Mark's appendix rupturing on the afternoon of a crucial statistics exam. I gave up the exam. Doug's rather fatherly lecture on that *B* I made later on the dreaded exam. "You're limited to one phone call per week. No more powwows with your friends. From now on leave that homemade bread and those cookies here for the starvation victims of your own malnourished household. Get up at three instead of four to hit the books!"

But such pride in the eyes of my little neighbor as she looked up at me and sighed, "Gosh, Mrs. Thrash, you're the best educated mentally retarded teacher I know of anywhere!"

And then my added bonus—three whole days off before I began the fall teaching term!

But mothers of the world who aspire to be middle-aged coeds, hear this. It can be done! Too often we encourage each other in mediocrity instead of opening up the valve of our generators. Bring that adventure drive out of the mothballs. Tap your hidden energies; rid yourself of self-maintaining tensions. Vaccinate yourself against self-pity and empty-nest jitters! Drinking at the Springs of Eternal Youth will make you as giddy as a spring day.

HE WAS A LEGEND . . .

"Dean Cate was a legend in the hills of East Tennessee. With his life hanging by a thread from day to day, he walked with death as if it were an acquaintance, a companion whom he recognized but did not fear."

Sitting quietly in the college chapel at my father's memorial service, I heard only a few of the eulogies. Snatches of off-key operas, merry brown eyes, and a hearty chuckle kept interrupting. Softly I heard his gentle voice reciting Walt Whitman's ode to Abraham Lincoln, "When Lilacs Last in the Doorway Bloomed," then "There's no fool like an educated fool." "You will always be the Dean's daughter, but remember, you're something special to your daddy!"

Salty tears, held back during the funeral, trickled down my cheeks as in the distance the last note of "Taps" wafted into nothingness. Never would my children meet Plato, Aristotle, or Socrates in the pumpkin patch as I had. They would never make these magical trips of childhood on their grandfather's strong shoulders.

One would have mistaken my father for a farmer, gardener,

or janitor—anything but a brilliant educator. He wore his farming outfit with greater ease than an educator's garb. Tilling the soil was his favorite pastime. It never talked back or asked foolish questions. How I loved to swoop down through the pumpkin patch, and on my daddy's shoulders weave in and out of the corn shocks as he hummed off-key bits of *Rigoletto* and *Faust* and muttered about the devil.

Second only to the soil was his ministry to rural churches. After rubbing noses in the intellectual world all week, he wanted to be among his own on Sunday. He was more at home in a rural kitchen over corn bread and milk than at a banquet table.

A captain-chaplain in the Army Reserve, my father was a deeply patriotic man; he would have had some choice words and facial contortions for flag-stompers! He never lost an opportunity to impress upon us our God-given rights and responsibilities as a citizen of the United States. There were tears swimming in his eyes as we jumped into his arms at a custom's gate in the New York Harbor. "I wanted to leap off that ship and wrap my arms around that Lady of Liberty as we passed! I've seen so much poverty, misery, little children sleeping in the streets and begging for bread . . . ." His staunch political views caused much merriment on the campus but I've lived to see his predictions come true.

My father loved his college with a passion. It was his life, his energy. He blazed an intellectual trail second to none! Judgment day in the Dean's office was a never-to-be-forgotten experience. One young woman of impeccable character was summoned one afternoon. One the verge of a nervous breakdown, she was told very solemnly by a twinkled-eyed dean that she was failing campusology!

A rich matron stormed the office demanding to know why her spoiled son had been kicked out and why the college couldn't reform him. After listening for an hour in silence, my father bored into her with those keen eyes, "Madame, you've had your son for eighteen years. Don't expect us to do in four months what you haven't done in eighteen years!" He then ushered her out of the "inner sanctum."

My favorite story of his forbearance happened on a Saturday night. It seems we always had hot dogs, potatoes, and pork and beans—these were standard fare. One night he didn't touch those pork and beans. What was the matter? When my mother asked if he weren't feeling well, he replied, "I feel fine. It's just that I've been eating these pork and beans for nineteen years and I never did like those things!"

I noted a faltering in my father's walking when I introduced him to his first grandson. Later it worsened and was diagnosed as muscular dystrophy. As the pains and pangs became more evident, he remained calm and undaunted, living Paul's motto, "In whatsoever state I am, therewith will I be content." Two years before death, he was told he had multiple sclerosis and only a few months to live. In the summer of 1954, he was flown to Denver to undergo extensive treatment and physical therapy.

"I'll never get to die of this disease. Those therapists will get me first!" Seeing the heart-hunger of people in the hospital, he organized a Bible class. He wrote me of this experience, "All those who attend are eager for the Word of God. I have Catholic and Jewish friends, even an agnostic. But I sit in the driver's seat and lay a firm hold on the reins!" My father never walked again.

He taught from his wheelchair, dismissing the inconvenience with, "I'm as good to my college from the neck up as I ever was. So far as my own personal infirmities are concerned, these old legs have carried me a long time in far places, and I have no doubt they'll carry me further."

I made a last visit with him after he returned from Denver so he could meet our wee daughter. He and his first grandson were inseparable; they began the day together at 5 A.M. Only when it was time to leave did the certainty engulf me.

How do you say earth's final farewell? I couldn't! I just flung my arms around that once-so-strong frame and willed him my strength as I whispered, "Daddy, I love you!"

Four hours before his death the following Easter season, he asked to be driven to his old homeplace and the tiny church, then to his farm; he shook hands with all and told them goodbye. The curtain, the veil, was lifted, and the Savior came to carry across the grand old man with the tired legs.

When the early morning Knoxville paper carried an account of his death, one of the little farm boys burst into tears, "Why that can't be the preacher; we just seed him last night!"

He has no building, no shrine at the college he served for thirty-one years. He needs none. A bit of him is scattered to earth's far corners in the hearts of his students. And his incorrigibly human namesake has far more than her share of "The Dean" nestled deep inside her omnibus of genes!

CONFESSIONS OF MIZ LADY

I became Miz Lady to nineteen disadvantaged, disillusioned, displaced teenagers by no accident. Believe me, I earned the title and it took all of five months to do it! Some of my friends didn't recognize me by the end of said period, so the score was evened.

I stumbled unwittingly on this unclaimed, undeveloped treasure. The special education director in the city to which we were transferred called my husband's office long before I appeared on the scene and wanted to hire me—sight unseen; he'd heard high praise from my former boss. However, the director forgot to mention that his jewels had run off three teachers in four months—the last poor soul having a near fatal heart attack.

The second day of the new year I was greeted with the principal's sagacious words, "They're yours. But don't ever try to break up a fight. You didn't come here to get cut up!"

The only male teacher—small, wiry, and stationed strategically next door—became my best friend. He'd come from a violent school situation in a northern city. Odds were laid in the classroom 5-1 against my holding out the week!

There was Roberto —slight of build, muscles of steel, wrists encircled with wide black leather bands, piercing eyes never missing anything and shooting off sparks of resentment—or was it pure hate?

" 'Ole Bessie, she's wierd! Just sits and smiles and smiles. Never says a word."

"Marie hears voices all time. Answers 'em, too. Hums and rocks, rocks and hums."

"Bet ya ain't seen nothin' till Herschel shows up. Sez to tell ya he'll be here in a few days to look ya over!"

Twenty-one in all, ages fourteen to nineteen. Nineteen blacks, two whites, arriving in three shifts through the endless morning. Dear God, HELP! HELP!

My total stockpile of program materials consisted of nine discarded telephone directories and four Sears wish books. There were no books because the director didn't believe in them. Fervently I prayed that all twenty-one would never show up on the same morning!

On that first Thursday a small ray of hope dawned. I was slightly wounded in an unplanned skirmish with the white kingpin. Blood dripped from my middle knuckle. With no verbalization whatsoever, Felicia, the Big Mama of the group, wet a dingy, brown paper towel and very gently wiped the blood from my knuckle. This was a sign that no one liked what the white kingpin had done.

But by Friday I knew failure unlimited; they'd pulled out all the stops on me. Where was all that expertise on my part and undying loyalty and rapport bit I'd developed in those twelve retarded rejects in my old city?

The first big break in the stalemate occurred on the second Monday when Herschel dropped in to look me over. Oozing sensuality, he flexed his muscles and flopped down. Later he swaggered to the center ring for his one-man act of heckling. The air was electric. I couldn't ignore the problem hoping it would go away. This was not a minor skirmish; it was the WAR! If I lost, those kids would laugh me right out the door, and they'd bring on the next victim. Quietly I delivered an ultimatum to Herschel, looking him straight in the eye. He chose not only to ignore it but to give me a good shove for extra measure. Matter-of-factly I put a water safety death grip on a startled Herschel and carted him unceremoniously the short distance to the principal's office. Then I all but fainted, realizing the risk I'd taken. Reentering the room, I walked to center stage and eyeballed my crew. "Are there any questions about who's boss?" There were none.

"I don't give a hoot about the color of your skin. You could be Purple People Eaters for all I care! (nervous twitter as eyeballs returned to sockets). But I do care about what's underneath that skin. Don't ever forget that! And because I do care, you're not going to run over me and you're not going to run me off! There are some rules of the game. You're going to make them for this room and since you'll make them, you're going to live by them. Are there any questions?" There were none. The odds shifted in my favor, so the grapevine reported that day.

My first problem was Roberto. Ridiculous as it seemed, he was the only student I had ever feared. Soon he would sense this, and there would be no progress. Aha! Grasping vocabulary and retaining it was his thing, so why not capitalize on this?

"Roberto, how did you get in this school?"

Black leather bands contracted, jaws tightened as he spat

out, "Don't know! They up and took me out of my junior high and threw me in this fallin' down retarded dump. I ain't retarded! I hate this dump and these retardos!"

"Maybe I can help you back to your junior high if you will help me. Do you want me to give you the word list a week early so you can get busy on it?" He said he'd like that. "By the way, Roberto, a guy next door called me dirty names and said he was going to beat me up first chance he got. I need a body guard."

From that day forward he was my protector. During any prolonged disagreement Roberto would rise up, flex his muscles, glare at the poor culprit, and announce, "Ya heard what The Lady said!" When asking anything of me, he always addressed me as Miz Lady.

Our self-styled curriculum consisted of functional math, vocabulary-language development, and social studies, which took in anything they wanted to discuss with me. I bombarded the bulletin board with pictures of souped-up cars of every description. The boys and I did math by figuring out the list price of each set of wheels, then we branched out into sales tax, down payment, interest rates, monthly payments, upkeep costs, bills, credit, debt, insurance, savings accounts, loan sharks, budgets, you name it! I coordinated job training, vocabulary, and math skills.

"Jerry, suppose you find you're spending too much money each week to meet your monthly car payment. Knowing they'll repossess it, what could you cut out?"

"Hmm! Oh, yeah! I been taking my gal out on Toosday nite and Satady, too. No mo' that Toosday night stuff unless she pays for it!"

My girls would take $100 shopping sprees in the wish book. "Plan your spring wardrobe. Who can get the most for their money?" Marie would interrupt her rocking and humming to buy clothes. We furnished houses, bought baby clothes, and did next year's Christmas shopping. The boys were very curious about the girls' wardrobes. They'd get up and peek at what the girls were buying. One day John pointed to a corset and remarked, "My mama has one of them contraptions to hold her in!"

Thursday's math always came from the grocery ads. Roberto had his best workout when tempers flared. Each Friday we planned an imaginary "Saturday Nite Blast" that would have killed off all the nutritional experts.

I taught my troops every word they might need to get any type of job. Many of their expressions would hinder them in getting or keeping a job, so we figured out another way to say the same thing. Many would copy this from the board. Always I respected their homes and their culture.

The boys loved to role play; all wanted to be boss. Boss always propped his feet on the desk, leaned back, and somehow looked far too relaxed to be boss!

One day one of the boys slipped up and used an old phrase. Off that desk came boss's feet. Boss ushered James right out the door with this admonition, "Boy, go home, wash your mouth out with soap, and come back tomorrow at 10!"

A teacher should not have favorites, but Joseph, breathing contagious joy and rhythm, was mine. During job training on courtesy, I asked a question from the one book I'd managed to lay my hands on. The unit was courtesy on the job. "If you saw someone fall down, what would be the first thing you'd do?"

Joseph's hand flew up while a foot tapped rhythmically. "First off I'd laugh awhile and den I'd rush over and ask, 'Is you hurt?' "

Their absolute honesty and vulnerability was priceless.

By March, our two white teenagers, having turned sixteen, had departed for far greater excitement; occasionally they saluted us on motorcycle runs. In the middle of the month I announced that my class would have their year-end blast at my home (always a tradition in my teaching). "But you must earn that privilege. Some of you better shape up because all go or no one goes!" I never bribed my class; we were straight shooters with each other. Peer discipline, the greatest thing I had going, was great because they loved to attend to each other's behavior. When the lid threatened to blow off, someone would always come up with, "Do you want US to go to Miz Lady's house or don't you?"

Early one afternoon we were jarred from our busy hum by an invasion—three toughs from next door climbing through our window. My "best friend" was often called to settle uprisings in other parts at which time his own toughs had a field day. With lightning speed I perceived this was another WAR. I had to win it, but I also had Roberto. Coldly, I eyeballed the invaders until they dropped their eyes. Static all but crackled in that charged atmosphere.

"In *our* room we have a door. (Roberto sat by the door.) We use that door. You gentlemen go right back out that window and if you have any business to conduct with us, come to the door and be received!"

Sullenly, for thirty seconds that lasted an hour, they sized me up. Roberto began flexing his muscles. The invaders departed through the window. My own troops let out a wail of protests! "Miz Lady, why'd ya call them ole dogs gentlemens? Why, they ain't no gentlemens!"

Something was troubling Roberto. Angry, moody, he'd been in three fights outside our domain. Only once did I have to get my "best friend" and that was the morning Marie had teased and thrown herself at Roberto and he all but put her through the wall that separated our rooms. Roberto brought his ball bat to school on a Tuesday because ours was broken. A not-too-smart tough decided to have some fun on the bus and take the bat away from Roberto. Roberto clobbered him in the head with the bat! The accurate grapevine reported the boy was bleeding quite a bit and Roberto was being held in the office. Sudden intution alerted me that I was going to get Roberto gift-wrapped for the day. Frantically I asked the class who was the best speller? Vocabulary guy? Runner-up to Joseph in last week's contest? "Roberto."

"Troops, you know Roberto is in some kind of trouble. No, we're not going to discuss that now. I have a feeling Roberto will be coming back to class soon. (Protestations.) Now don't you dare say a word to him. Don't bump him; don't even go by his desk. He gets a vacation all day. He's been working too hard so he doesn't have to do anything today. Yes, if you work that hard, I'll give you a goof-off day. Do you understand?"

Exactly three minutes later Roberto appeared—livid with rage and muttering to himself. After briefly patting him on the shoulders and feeling vibrations, I didn't "see" Roberto the rest of the day. We ignored him as we went out to lunch. He looked at me, but I didn't "see" him. The 2:15 bus blast was sweeter than any cathedral chime.

After that when black moods engulfed him—he had a badly deformed baby brother—he'd announce, "Miz Lady, I gotta take a little vacation from this dumb school! I'll be up in Zeph Hills; be back in two days." I could have set a sundial by the hour he said he'd return.

Bessie was my unfolding miracle. Her seat work was beautiful, accurate; but she spoke only yes and no. Outdoors I studied her carefully; she internalized everything that went on about her and responded nonverbally or in monosyllables. I began by sitting by her for fifteen-minute stretches in class. I went over every paper she did, praising her generously, patting her on the back. Then I'd open the wish book and ask if she liked this outfit or that. I carried on such an animated conversation that my boys whispered that I was getting retarded, too. Bessie nodded and smiled, but those beautiful eyes! How they talked to me. They danced in merriment, dropped modestly at compliments, widened in curiosity, and clouded with empathy! In early May as I sat with Bessie, I sifted the fabric of her pretty dress through my fingers and asked where she'd bought it. The most beautiful smile I've ever seen broke out as she looked up to me and said, "My mother made it." Tear after tear streamed down my salty cheeks. I was done for the day. My boys taught math and social studies. The grapevine report that day: "Bessie's a talkin' and Miz Lady's a bawlin'!"

We always did things up in a big way, and the year-end blast at my house was no exception. A stalled hurricane blew in on the big day. I awoke to the thud of driving rain and the groaning and swaying of our palms. Willard was in New Orleans and Houston that week so I couldn't lean on his quiet sanity that sustained me in so many of my self-inflicted disasters. Bless him. He dismissed most of them with the off-hand explanation, "Your mother is a remarkable woman!"

None of the troops were absent that sloppy morning. In fact, I found an extra—one of the window invaders. "Alfredo, you nut. Sneakin' in here thinkin' yu was a goin' to teacher's house! Git out!" The bouncer of the week escorted him through the door! It never dawned on my troops to ask if we were still going. After all, a promise is a promise!

Shortly before noon I screwed up my courage and ambled into the office. Quite casually handing my principal the permission slips I remarked, "Here are all the slips." My principal stared at me, unbelieving—his jaw dropped, his mouth flew open, and out tumbled a lengthy tirade.

I listened sweetly. My turn. "Sir, do you know how long ago I promised my kids this party? Since last March—count it up. Not one parent has called in this morning and canceled out. (Nervously, I'd checked with the secretary all morning.) That hurricane isn't due in until 9:30 tonight, and I'll have every kid back by 6!"

His countenance took on that dazed, spaced-out look I've often noted on my husband's mug. "Besides," and I delivered my trump card as I eyeballed him, "A promise is a promise!"

In high spirits we sloshed through four inches of rain to my abode. Older son swung the garage doors open, and in we trooped! "Well, hello there, grandfather! Pleezed to meet ya. How ya doin' today?" George even kissed grandfather clock.

First off, as Joseph would say, there was a tour of the house. They touched, cradled, caressed, oohed, and aahed! Next everyone took a turn on the piano. Then the best part! Their kind of music and eats that would have killed off the nutritional experts! They'd planned the menu. My own four served and every so often a "Waiter, fill 'er up again" could be heard. There was no color or class distinction that afternoon. We were all Purple People Eaters.

At 5:15 they announced, "Seein' as how ya husban' is gone and ya might get lonesome and skeered tonight, we'll just bed down and keep ya company!"

"That hurricane is really churning up, and I promised your mamas I'd have every one of you home by 6. And a promise is a promise! Now grab your things and tell grandfather goodbye!" There was no more discussion and all were delivered by 6.

Since stumbling upon my "African Treasure," I've taught other classes, created and coordinated a multilevel program for trainables, supervised university interns, and taught nursing seminars. Somehow my methodology instructions always comes back to those lessons of the heart I learned from that class.

On arising each morning I see the musical notes Bessie made for me before she spoke. Each tiny grain of orange rice was placed on those wooden notes with only a toothpick and Elmer's glue. A pottery masterpiece, a "Glad You Is My Teacher" gift graces my dresser. If I could take it with me, these would go!

Months after this experience I was summoned to the principal's office. (I still go with fear and trembling!) "Tell me your secret," he implored. "I've been down your wing when every other class was in chaos. But I've never seen your class unglued or you all fired up!" (This was on a day when racial incidents had flared, and "Mama hen" and her eleven-year-old banty roosters had made KEEP YOUR COOL signs and worn them all day.)

"It's really no secret, and it didn't come from me. It's very, very old; given by the Master Teacher. The Golden Rule. Reverence for personality. I treat those kids like they were very special. And they are! They don't ever want to let me down!"

The love chapter describes it. "If you love someone you will always be loyal to him no matter what the cost. You will always believe in him, always expect the best of him, and always, stand your ground in defending him" (1 Cor. 13:7, TLB). Love never gives up!

NOSEGAY TO GRANNY

Thank you for giving your life for the one I chose in marriage. He was your only one, but you released him long before "Lohengrin's" echoes. You entrusted him to me, thereby freeing yourself of jealousy, possessiveness.

Thank you for loving his father openly, tenderly—for sending him off each day with a big kiss. Therein you taught a son sustaining love and affection—whatever may come.

Thank you for making gentleness and courtly manners

part of a son's upbringing. Though he had no sister on which to practice, you reminded him to treat each young lady as he would have wanted his sister treated—had she lived.

Thank you for giving him confidence in himself and his ability to succeed. Though circumstances limited your formal education, you refused to pass on any such limitation to him. "You can do anything you set your mind to doing," was your philosophy.

Thank you for sparing him emotional indulgences. Pain, loss, heartbreak were glued into your marriage, but you permitted no self-pity, no pessimism to corrode his potential.

Thank you for telling everyone I was a much better cook than you, although your pot roasts, potato salad, and spaghetti sauce put me to shame! (I forgive your not teaching him to eat carrots without complaint.)

Thank you for the priceless heritage of a firsthand faith in a living, dependable God.

Thank you for a mother's love that glows through the years—sharing our burdens, hurts, and participating in our happy anticipations.

HANG IN THERE!

I did not wait for the five-year summons from my class president bidding me to our Carson-Newman class reunion. In joyful anticipation of my brief sabbatical from my superactive family, I cashed in my Medicare coupons and purchased my plane ticket from St. Petersburg, winter home of the Cardinals and half the retired people.

A week before D-Day, my three sons began their own brand of Alka Seltzer commercials and complaints about dining on Diane's disasters.

I told my principal I needed two days of sick leave since I was sick and tired of school. (One of the fringe benefits of being a "mentally-retarded teacher" is occasionally naming your own terms without reason.)

"Are you coming back?" he inquired anxiously, tearing out the remaining bit of thatch upon his roof.

"Not if I get a better offer," I replied sweetly.

Thursday was almost a typical day. I left for school before 7 A.M., taught seventy pupils, then fled school with my children. After driving the hundred blocks home, I cast myself in the salt water for my aqua jogging. Next I hurried for my annual appointment with the hairdresser.

Upon seeing the "new me," my wise old twelve-year-old blurted, "Motheeeeer, how much starch did that guy put in your hair?" Oh, well, you can't win them all! Besides, I did get a lot of mileage from that $3.50 hairdo!

At 6:30 P.M. I waved good-bye to one sinking husband and boarded my flight, taking an assigned seat next to a bearded and mustached young man who resembled Moses and Father Flanagan wrapped in one package. To my amazement we communicated quite well, and he appeared to be unaware of my advancing vintage.

Friday morning found me in chapel—yes, they still have this ritual—hearing an exciting address by Dr. Harry Laws. I felt guilty only a couple of times when he spoke of overpopulation on Planet Earth. I had contributed a bit more than my 1.7 child; actually, that .7 of a child has always puzzled me a bit. Dr. Laws concluded his scholarly address with an unexpected, "Hang in there, young people! Stay with it!" Believe me, little did he know how long I *had* been hanging on and in. With three teenagers and one on deck, you roll with the punches.

A Saturday sun dazzled the crisp fall foliage. I rushed up to the old administration building and I scanned the horizon for "fortyish" people who had symptoms of comatic chromosomes and collapsing cells. However, that old eagle atop our prized monument (toward which I contributed my last $2.00) looked a lot more tired than any of us.

The alumni luncheon was delicious, although I was sure there wasn't a turkey left in East Tennessee. At least we solved the overpopulated turkey problem.

We arrived at the football stadium along with the ambulance and rescue squad. I wasn't too sure whether the attendants came for us or the players.

All the Saturday night confessions at our reunion would have overjoyed a parish priest. Alas! Dan Carroll, returned missionary from South America, confessed Spanish was the only subject he'd ever failed. Richard Lucas remarked they just weren't making these desk seats as large as in the olden days, then owned up to having gained fifty pounds. One maiden acknowledged, "I was Bettye Jean Cooper. I still am Bettye Jean Cooper." Bob Provost divulged he had begun delivering second generation babies in Mississippi, and this raised the question in his mind of prime or decline.

One of our long-suffering professors just happened to wander in at photo time to make a sly remark about those "back-row baldies" just like him. Come to think of it, the waves had departed from several beaches.

One veteran couple actually admitted to having a sophomore at the college. None boasted of grandparentage, and all the millionaires stayed at home to count their filthy lucre.

As for me, I confessed to having finally found my niche in history—in the field of mental retardation. I was always brain-damaged in math, but an extra touch of insanity is a real asset in my field. Come each Friday and I'm a psychological mishap!

The final confession of the night came from a gal who'd received her proposal of marriage on the back steps of Henderson Hall. "Courting posterity was dealt a serious blow with the demolition of 'Hen Hall,' but I have three bricks from it in our fireplace. I carried my memories with me!"

As that harvest moon winked on East Tennessee, our happy group scattered to the four winds. One classmate declared he fully expected me to have been to the moon and back before our next "happening." Another insisted I bring my husband to the next roundup because he wished to have a peek at this remarkable man who'd managed to live with me for lo these many years.

Instant rejuvenation engulfed me as I winged back to my decompression chamber. I pondered over why some people were old at forty and others ageless at eighty. Couldn't the difference be laughter, love, and contagious enthusiasm for life? I actually expect something exciting to happen each day, and my family and circumstances seldom let me down.

My conclusion, penned in haste amid wall-to-wall people in this Atlanta airport, is somewhat less than profound. Youth is still an internal state of mind, a nostalgia for the future. And the best is yet to be!

Now let me see if I can predict what Willard is going to say when he sees me alight from the plane clutching this huge half of a maple tree from my old front yard.

ODE TO PA PA

He left us on a Sunday afternoon in November—this gallant Pa Pa—two hours before his only son reached his bedside. Nine years of battling cancer—then the worn heart gave up. They laid him gently beside his infant son and daughter, victims of typhoid, who never knew their soft-spoken father.

My husband stood tall at his father's funeral and reminded us that, although Pa Pa would have never won any church-attendance rewards, he daily lived the Sermon on the Mount. Gentleness, going the second mile, nonretaliation, living each day as it came without borrowing tomorrow's troubles, nonjudgment, and accepting people as they were became a way of life with him. He was the Gulf Stream of his family, warming each heart with genuine concern. "Pa Pa was the world's greatest listener!"

Knowing this quiet, gentle Pa Pa made our hearts understand why God chose Bethlehem, not Rome; a manger, not a throne; the cross, not a crown; and this world's obscure, not the mighty.

On this December night, boat carolers, shattering the stillness of our waterway with "O Come All Ye Faithful," remind us of Pa Pa's visit with us last Christmas. His very first plane flight—what a happening. All the relatives called long distance to hear of his adventure. And he, not Granny, told them all about it!

Gently I lift the tiny, white snowbird that graced his Christmas tree for thirty years before it became ours. Pa Pa knew the heights and depths of life. He left a legacy of goodwill to all men. "He shall be like a tree planted by the rivers of water, that bringeth forth his fruit in his season" (Ps. 1:3).

WILLIAM'S RAISE

One of my heart memories of William, who died last week of a massive brain tumor, was his request for a pay raise.

Twenty-one-year-old William timidly approached the ceramics director early one Wednesday afternoon after he'd received his pay envelope.

"Mrs. Byrd, may I talk to you?"

"Certainly, William. What's on your mind?"

"Mrs. Byrd, I just got to have a raise!"

"Oh, Well, William, why do you need a raise?"

"Well, Mrs. Byrd, it's like this. I have to support my mother and my sister, and I just can't do it any more on what I make!"

"Hmm. William, let's see. How much do you make each week?"

"Seventy-five cents, Ma'am."

"And how much do you think you'll need to make each week to support your mother and sister?"

"Oh, I think a dollar a week would do it nicely."

"William, I can't just give it to you because you need it. Do you think you could earn that raise?"

"Oh, yes ma'am! I'll sweep up this shop every afternoon!"

"Good! It's a deal then. You've got yourself a raise!"

William burst excitedly into my office next door. "Guess what, Mrs. Thrash, I got a raise! I'm making a dollar a week now!"

I chuckled inwardly as he told me all the details. Then William's reasoning sobered me. How like William I am! I approach the Giver of all gifts, whose coffers are full and overflowing, and I timidly ask him for a 25-cent raise.

"You have not because you ask not."

GRANDMOTHER—SECOND ONLY TO SOLOMON!

"Who was the wisest person in the whole world?" Ask my

children that and the answer is prompt and convincing.

"Solomon, but my grandmother would run him a close second!"

"Grandmother Cate is swift! She can hoof it to the top of Clingman's Dome, and she's ridden everthing in California Disneyland. I bet she'll be the first person in Jefferson City to go to the moon!"

"Why, Grandmother invented recycling and ecology economy. For years she's recycled everything but us. And I think she was tempted to do that on plenty of occasions!"

"Grandmother Cate is as sharp as Perry Mason and Ironside put together. And you'd better not yak during their sleuthing when you're at Grandmother's!"

My four offspring think Grandmother hung the moon. My husband declares her the world's greatest mother-in-law, although I've long suspected those thick Charlie Brown volumes she gives him each birthday influence the situation. As for me, I'm pleased to have this gallant lady as my mother.

"To be successful you must pick your ancestors with care," quipped my favorite psychology professor. Well, we really picked a winner in our household.

In a day of vanishing absolutes, Grandmother is something special. She's moved with the times. Yet those old-fashioned virtues of integrity, faith, and hard work are an integral part of her life.

Her insatiable quest for knowledge has been a constant inspiration to our household. Rigor mortis of the mind is unheard of with Grandmother, although she's passed the three score and ten. "I could spend a month in Grandmother's library and hardly make a dent."

"I love to go to Grandmother's. She isn't a fussy housekeeper. So what if the beds don't get made each morning; we're going to crawl right back in that night, anyway. Friendly dust, clutter, and Grandmother are very compatible.

She's got far more important things to do than win a *Good Housekeeping* award!"

"There is one small flaw in Grandmother," one of the four admitted. "She works too hard and she sorta thinks everybody enjoys it that much!"

She has boundless good health and energy. Occasionally she sleeps to the "late" hour of 7 A.M. before she's up and at it in her garden, yard, basement, on her farm, or reading. "Grandmother won't ever come unglued!"

After unexpected but serious surgery, Grandmother awoke to find all the interns leaning over her bed and gawking. The surgeon was remarking, "Now my patient claims to be over sixty-five, but her constitutional makeup is that of a thirty-five-year-old.

When the doctor released her, telling her to go home and do a normal day's work, she did just that. An anxious neighbor who was a nurse came the next morning to find Grandmother cruising about. "But did that doctor know what your *normal* day included?" she inquired incredibly.

Another time Grandmother checked into the local hospital for an overnight stay to have some tests run before taking off for distant shores. A flu epidemic had slowed hospital service to a snail's pace. Grandmother took one look at that limp gelatin they brought her. Then she discarded her hospital attire, put on her street clothes, strolled casually out, went home, and leisurely ate supper. Then she returned to don her hospital garb. When on-duty nurses finally figured it out, they all but fainted on the spot!

One year Grandmother and her sister-in-law drove to Miami to spend the Christmas holidays with us. Snow was predicted throughout Tennessee and all the way to Atlanta. When her neighbor came over to help put chains on the car, he admonished her about starting out at 4 A.M. the next morning in a snowstorm. "Kindly help me get the chains on and keep your opinions to yourself!" was her reply.

"My grandmother's a real hot-rodder," says Mark. "Riding with her is more exciting than going down that first hump on the roller coaster!"

"Yes, we spend more time under the seat than on it," confesses Diane. "One holiday season my grandmother left at 4 A.M. (her magic departure hour) and drove to St. Petersburg before the sun went down. She had an hour's siesta on the patio while my mother fixed supper. Then, would you believe, she went to the midnight sale with us to buy our Christmas tree?"

"Did Grandmother ever wallop you?" David asked. You bet she did! She didn't exactly rear us with a psychology book in one hand and a behavior modification sheet in the other. Grandmother had her own tried and trusty method of modifying unacceptable behavior. If appealing to reason didn't work the first or second time, she appealed to the other extremity. Oh, yes! Discipline was painful for the moment, but my psyche was never damaged. And she never gave us any of that "This-hurts-me-more-than-it-does-you" bit. We couldn't play Grandmother against Granddaddy. She caught on to that. She was also consistent. We didn't get away with mischief one time and get punished for the same act another time.

I remember how well she vented her righteous indignation after returning from Knoxville one afternoon. She found her ancient oil painting (of ships at sea) severely wounded from a neighborhood spitball battle in our living room! During the warming-up period of reckoning over that trespass, she called out, "What are you yelling for? I haven't even hit you yet!"

Grandmother's most admirable quality to her grandchildren is her tenacity of spirit. After picking bushels of blackberries on the farm, David lamented, "Grandmother won't let you be a quitter!" Giving up is not in her makeup.

Her backbone is stronger than her wishbone.

According to her, God didn't build fences around Christians and erect a KEEP OUT sign. Bad breaks come to everyone, and you can choose to sit down and whine, "Why did this happen to me?" and lick your wounds, or use your gumption to roll with the punches and come out on top.

"If you make a mistake," she reasoned, "analyze it, learn something from it, and use it as a stepping-stone to a wiser, more intelligent decision next time."

Our eldest practices Grandmother's tenacity of spirit when life caves in on him at the Naval Academy. "I won't throw in the towel! You can take anything as long as you take it only one day at a time!" is his philosophy.

Grandmother gives without remembering. She never counts the cost or reminds you of what she's done. Concern for things, with no strings attached, is her life-style.

One of my special childhood memories was running the Christmas cake route with her. Mr. Crooke always rated a fluffy thirteen-egg angel food cake with red cherries strewn about the seven-minute icing. Another shut-in received the caramel pecan delight and on and on. Grandmother remembered people who could not return favors. There was no thought of exchange. "To give with no thought of return; that's what makes it a gift."

The gift of a grateful heart is also Grandmother's. Little things made her the happiest. In memory I can still see the mist in those blue eyes as I hunted the first cluster of spring violets and pressed them in her hand with a shy smile. When she awoke from her siesta (she invented this sanity saver) in the summer, I served her iced lemonade. She thanked me as though I'd brought heavenly nectar.

The gift I so admire in Grandmother is her ability to sort values and establish priorities. She never spends first-rate energy on second-rate things. She knows how to be happy in doing without. She gives up certain luxuries (not necessities) in order to afford more rewarding ones.

Traveling is her one big luxury. She has climbed the highest mountains, crossed and recrossed seas, deserts, and jungles. Yet she has paid the price of giving up something of lesser value for this pearl of great price. I can hear her now, "Debt is the oldest form of human bondage." One of the few times we've ever seen Grandmother angry was the day some car salesman stuck a notice on her windshield reminding her her car was four years old, promising her excellent interest rates on a new one. "I am certainly capable of knowing when *I* need a new car and how I will pay for it," she fumed!

Grandmother's secret in life is her wellspring of deep spiritual reserve. Barnacles will never crust over her heart nor will arthritis of the soul overtake her. Simplicity and serenity of spirit are hers. "God didn't call you to orbit the earth but to inhabit it."

Grandmother doesn't issue edicts from ivory towers. She's right there in the arena of life rubbing shoulders with the touchables and the untouchables. She accepts and appreciates people for whatever they are, not what she'd like for them to be. Her quiet dignity and unpretentious life-style inspire a college community.

One of the deepest regrets of my life is not having told my father how much he meant to me. With gratitude and deep humility I want to tell my gallant mother that she is very special even though mere words are inadequate.

Twinkling eyes, dry wit, practicality, infectious laughter, humility, spiritual dynamo!

"What's more fun than confetti and fireworks on the Fourth of July?"

"My Grandmother," echoes our brood. "And you haven't lived until you've met her!"

I COULDN'T PRAY

Out of the depths I cry, but I am inarticulate. No voice, no language can express my grief, my numbness of shock. It's like a death in our family, only there is no body to bury, no memorial service.

Our friend and co-worker betrayed my husband, did him in, spat out evil untruths, became as ragingly jealous as King Saul of old when he was consumed by the green-eyed monster of jealousy.

There was no discussion, no warning, no trial, no defense—just backdoor treachery as one man's exalted ego plotted against another man's good name, reputation, and livelihood! Had we been living in Russia or Cuba or China, I could have understood this and accepted it, but not here in this city, Lord. How can Christians behave toward one another like this?

My husband, the dearest one on earth to me, is dazed, silent, broken in spirit. He did not retaliate; he demanded no hearing, but I have an itch to act, to shout to the world this gross injustice.

How do you explain such a betrayal to your children? How do you tell them your co-worker couldn't take our family's success? With half truths? My husband never mentioned our friend's name. "I cannot do this to our children," was his simple reply. "We will rise above this and time will tell in a way we never can."

Dear husband, don't quote Psalm 37 to me; I don't want to hear it! God's reality is very distant right now. All I can fathom is man's inhumanity to man.

I sit in my closet and weep so the children can't hear. Deep racking sobs. "In everything give thanks." How can I give thanks for these heart scalds?

But I am not alone. Dear ones share our grief; they hurt

with us. A soft ring of the door bell, then my dearest friend rushes to my closet unannounced, throws her arms about me, and squalls with me. No hasty moralizing, no pep talks, no telling me to get hold of myself. Just a quiet "I don't understand it either."

Gradually the sobbing subsides. We do look a little silly huddled on the floor of my walk-in closet. After a discreet bit, our husbands peek into the closet. One of them quotes, "And when you enter your closet to pray . . . ." I shoot back, "I don't think the Lord is interested in what I have to say to him right now!" With faltering steps we grasp outstretched hands and leave our vigil of grief.

What can I do with this? How can I use it? Again and again I slip away to ponder, shutting out the noise of the world and listening quietly to the deeper guidance from my inner citadel. "Faith is absolute trust in God as to the outcome no matter how dark the picture . . . . No human experience need be a liability . . . . You give other people a lot of power when you allow their comments to shape your life . . . . Forgive even as I forgave you . . . . I will go with you all the way."

Still later. "You can't get ahead by getting even. Haven't you wallowed in self-commiseration long enough? Be honest! Isn't your seed of self-concern, your bruised ego the main object of your grief?"

Beauty from ashes. Slowly, silently life's balance is restored. Gradually I awaken. "O God, I don't understand this. It hurts worse than if someone had done me in. But you didn't cause it; sin did. I can only accept the fact that it has happened, and you can bring good out of anything if we trust in you to see us through. I know that intellectually— help me to accept it emotionally.

Your kingdom is from within, although we allow external forces to shake it up. I want to rise again; the children have seen me so fragmented, so torn apart. I've been so engrossed in grief and self-pity, I've forgotten all those occasions when my joy was so great, I could not articulate it. Thank you for all those times. I can't honestly give thanks for this experience just yet, but someday I will be able to. Don't allow this unfortunate spirit to fester. Heal my wound clean—one day at a time!"

"The Lord is near to those who are brokenhearted."

FROM ADAM TO NOW

Since Eden's garden when Adam, the first electronics engineer, furnished spare parts for the first loudspeaker, there has been a running battle of the wills. "Lord, this woman made me do it!"

As I ponder Women's Lib, the latest invention in the age-old battle, I must confess I have more liberation than I know how to handle most of the time!

Methinks "Mine" and "Thine" have divided more homes, soured more relationships, and caused more lawsuits than this world has ever dreamed.

God made us male and female to complement each other, not to compete with one another, and viva la difference! Alas, most of our misunderstandings in the husband-wife department have come from competing with each other. In marriage it's not equal power but equal loving, cherishing, honoring, and sharing that count. As my brother penned me, "It seems so simple and would lead to such bliss. But it seems we have too much selfishness and are too busy 'thinking of our own rights.' "

I have no desire to be addressed as "Ms." I need a master, a head of the household. I come from a long line of headstrong women, and I need someone to wave a verbal stick and good-naturedly growl, "Enough, enough!" Moreover, I need all the help I can get. Offspring are so adept at sensing the absence of an authority figure. Having sensed it, they lose no time in driving a wedge between parents, playing one against the other, and the home splits, although all may continue to exist together. Such behavior tracks make patterns in children's minds, and they often repeat the same mistakes in their marriages. Passive dads often reproduce passive sons. Authoritative mothers reproduce daughters with like behavior traits. They imitate their models.

It's true, I've been passed over in my profession and a position given to a male who didn't have my education or expertise. But you never promised us life would be fair. I've chafed awhile until I realized "I'm a child of the King," and my Father will always provide a challenge.

You played no favorites, Savior. You came to save us from ourselves—so often our own worst enemy. You had women disciples! Dr. Luke tells us they went from village to village with you and the twelve ministering to the people. Many other women contributed to your support from their private purses! (A first-century WMU.) I guess women have always had private purses!

Early that glorious Easter morn the first person to see you was Mary Magdalene. "Why are you crying?" you asked her tenderly. Then "Mary." Not a gossamer dream, a haunting memory, but reality! That garden couldn't contain her! Master, you knew she would go and tell! And women have been telling others about you since.

You gave me all the liberation I needed when you promised, "I have come to give you life in all its fullness." Your abundance knows no sex discrimination.

Part III
Emptying the Nest

And his mother stored away all
these things in her heart.

FOOTFALLS

Tiny, you tug at apron strings; tall, you tie up heartstrings!

> Once we rocked, sang, touched a fevered brow, comforted a troubled dreamer.

> We listened to the telltale rattle, breathed the nightly vapor fumes, cringed at the rasping wheeze, inhaled the loneliness of an empty bed without its familiar boy.

Then you grew older. We sighed! Ah, unbroken rest, relief, relaxation!
But not for long.

> Now we listen for approaching cars, cringe at shrieking brakes, comfort each other that it's not our own.

> We touch and gently sigh as one by one you come home. A click at the door, telltale footfalls that identify each of you. A booming "I'm home" before the witching hour. With the last one in, we breathe a prayer of gratitude and inhale the remaining night.

Unbroken rest? No! Too big to hold on our laps, you're forever in our hearts!

HELP! WE'RE OUTNUMBERED!

"And Dear God, help us! Now that we have four teenagers in this house," Mark petitioned earnestly at breakfast on the day the spontaneous combusted! One daddy called his secretary of old in a distant city. "Cleo, you remember all that free advice I gave you when Debbie became a teenager? . . . Well, what did I advise? . . . Oh, you and Wilbur cry a lot and pray more often! . . . But we've been doing that already!"

Heeelp! We're outnumbered by all four of our contributions to the population explosion. Insanity could be hereditary; you might get it from your offspring! Anyone inventing a vaccine for adolescence could walk away with that Nobel Peace Prize.

These offshoots entertain and agonize us day and night with their quarreling, rumblings, homespun philosophy, and get-rich-quick schemes on how to be a millionaire by age eighteen! Could they have been innoculated with a Gramophone needle? I wonder if it's possible to guide your teens through those earthshaking maniac years without succumbing to mental derangement? One thing certain, children are not only a joy of old age; they contribute mightily to it!

Are there secrets of survival! I think so. Don't be thrown off balance by little pedestrian things (like long hair, my youngest would add!). Don't excite the blood. Sit loosely in the saddle. Don't look back; they may be gaining.

"Come ye apart" or come apart. We usually come apart,

but we need not! "Don't be anxious about tomorrow. God will take care of your tomorrows, too. Live one day at a time" (Matt. 6:34,TLB). We borrow so many of tomorrow's troubles that we can't operate in the today! But an all-wise God unfolds the future just one day at a time. That's the only way parents of teenagers can make it—one day at a time.

Living is an art, not an exact science. The home is still the laboratory. Our future is not frozen; it's for us to make—one day at a time. Let us and our teenagers not go faster than God. "Bring them up with loving discipline" (Eph. 6:4,TLB).

UNEXPECTED BONUS—THE JOY BOYS

Oh, delirious joy! "What a dingdong of a day!" I couldn't have stood those teachers another day!" Those glorious final hours of school had hurtled upon us. Those Joy Boys were something again!

Actually, we were members of the Unplanned Parenthood Generation. True, before being wedded we decided four kids would be our contribution to the population explosion—one of each variety with a spare to keep them company!

My doctor decreed otherwise, declaring I would never make my quota with a broken back and such irregular pelvic structure. He was right. I almost didn't make it! After one of each variety came a year of "repairs" and a "Don't-tempt-fate" admonition. Then lo and behold, while I was lying on a board in traction, I perceived that our family was not completed. Some months later in the dead heat of July, Joy Boy I made his entrance seven weeks ahead of schedule. Lung complications and yellow jaundice necessitated his remaining behind in an incubator. Then one glad day two parents, two kids, and one grandmother reclaimed Baby Brother.

A year later, lacking six days, Joy Boy II joined the scene prematurely. Mom and son remained in the hospital so long that nurses threatened to enroll son in the Baptist Hospital cradle roll. On the day we rejoined the home front, elder brother and sister took one peek, then promptly declared, "Let's get right back in the car and take him back and trade him in on a sister. We got a brother last year."

With four preschoolers and twins a year apart, I was ready to do some wide-scale trading or offer the children as door prizes! Joy Boy I would discard his bottle, steal brother's formula, prop his feet on the baby buggy (which by now rocked and sang "Brahm's Lullaby" with the slightest pressure), and guzzle brother's refreshment. Mom and Dad both had a baby to feed at mealtime. Dad forgot that so often that Joy Boy I learned to feed himself at the tenderest age known to mankind. Our first vacation was chaotic; we resembled a rolling baby furniture ad; at each sanity break, we let down the tailgate of the wagon and each parent changed his baby. By the next year Dad declared proudly, "I guess you know I have my baby out of diapers this year!"

I looked like a reject from a Siberian labor camp, and Dad did his share of hospital vigil by oxygen tents. We supported the local pediatrician monthly for the first five years.

Looking back, we really can't imagine life without our Joy Boys! How dull! How peaceful. The boys developed their own Tarzan-Cheetah gibberish; we had no idea what they were saying, but they understood each other perfectly. On David's third birthday—he lives for those six days he's the same age as Mark—we heard him bawling his heart out. "I'm the same age as Mark, and we're supposed to be the same size, and he's taller than me!"

Our Joy Boys had a natural affinity for dirt, creepy crawlers, combustion, and daring. Mark had a kitchen shelf alloted to him, and he banged and stacked pots and pans, creating his own educational toys. He chattered incessantly.

Everyone commented on how timid and quiet he was. I contended he was so worn out from rattling at home that he was bound to rest sometime, someplace! David, the family vet, rescued all the wounded birds, animals, and creepy crawlers. Once we happened upon him poking Vicks in Kitty's nose because she'd sneezed.

We separated them by rooms when we discovered David was doing all of Mark's math homework for 3 cents **per** day. Although one was fair-skinned and blue-eyed and the other dark-complexioned and brown-eyed, everybody confused them for they were inseparable. "I'm Mark and he's David," became a daily routine. "Do you suppose when one of us gets married, we'll still be saying, 'I'm David and he's Mark' "?

Years after they'd joined the family circus, Mark and Dave discovered one Friday night that all four kids would be attending one function or another. "Are you sure you'll be OK, Mother? You won't get lonesome, will you?" Their concern was so genuine, I had not the heart to tell them how long I'd waited for such an occasion.

Their favorite expression when I bomb out is, "Oh, that's OK. We'll give you ONE more chance! I calculate I've used up 2,396¼ chances as of this writing.

Each time I threaten to run away and join the gypsies before mealtime, Willard explains to me that thus/so is only a temporary stage of insanity/rebellion, or whatever, and that it can't last but 17½ more months. There's one big, fat headache connected with this. Just as Joy Boy I is completing this stage and I'm inert from overexposure, Joy Boy II is just commencing the phase.

"We'll have to wait twenty years before we know whether we've done something right," their daddy reminds me.

Twenty years! Perish the thought! I may not be around by then.

Dad's "chip-off-the-ole-block" button lighted up as Joy Boy II walked away with the "outstanding student of the

119

year" trophy in his elementary school, and both parents were dumbfounded this year at his No. 1 in the state in German comprehension award. We always knew this kid comprehended a language we didn't speak.

When Joy Boy II, clutching that big tennis trophy, strolled in from the yearly athletic banquet, our tennis genes rose to the surface and cheered. I could hardly believe this six-foot-three-inch bean pole was the same wheezy kid who stole his brother's formula and guzzled it down!

Overjoyed, I ventured the suggestion that we might not have to wait twenty years before knowing whether we did anything right. Guess who cautioned against over-optimism?

TO OUR PLEBE

Son, you were so curious that you zeroed in on your parents one full month before launching schedule. Peering at the world through those deep pools of sable, that shock of thick, black hair, you liked what you saw. For seventeen-and-a-half years you've lived life to the hilt and rolled with the punches! The prosperity of your spirit was unaffected by how little or how much your parents possessed. At an early age you realized how transitory money is. You enjoyed life in our ancient Alamo (Noah's Boat as we sometimes called it when the rains descended and your furniture floated) as much as our present waterfront motel.

As the oldest of four "stairsteps," you were the peacemaker—gentle and firm but no coward. When your daddy told you it was necessary to conquer the neighborhood bully, who daily lay in wait for you in the first grade and then gave you boxing lessons, you felled him with a couple of quick punches. Yet fighting was not your life-style. When others around you lost their cool, you hung onto yours! "Come now and let us reason together" was your way of operating.

Doug, your dad often remarked that you were born with an inner discipline and maturity. It was not necessary to surround you with gifts or load you with cumbersome advice. Even in preschool years, that computer in your brain investigated, sifted, analyzed, and evaluated situations. You never pretended superiority, paraded piety, or faked a stuffy goodness. Yet your ability to determine right was uncanny.

Work was no disgrace, and you never believed the world owed you anything. Since the age of thirteen you've had a job. You cleaned a church (including the debris of pigeons from the steeple), swept and polished a drugstore, pumped gas, stocked grocery shelves, and became an assistant dairy manager while carrying honor courses your senior year. Responsibility was never a stranger to you. Was it any wonder you were offered a full dairy managership by the time you were seventeen?

Your dad and I gave you the gift of freedom to be yourself, not some puny extension of our own egos. We allowed you to make your own mistakes. Believe me, some were whoppers! Somehow our whole household profited and matured with you from these honest errors.

Remember how furious your father was the night you accidentally reversed his Volks bug into that huge truck in the church parking lot? As afraid as you were, you went straight to his office and blurted out the news in his presence. It was a good thing he had finished his solos at that wedding! An entire church awaited with bated breath the outcome of your accident.

When your father overcame his anger and shock, he spoke: "What do you think we ought to do about this, Son?"

You meted out your own punishment. "I think I should have to pay all repair costs." I sizzled for two days when you took $100 from your savings and paid the bill. That represented 200 hours of janitorial labor! If I'd had the money, I probably would have given it to you and deprived you of the valuable lesson of accepting the consequences of your actions. Events at the "Threshold" were pretty sticky the next week with Bible school going on and no bug about! Somehow I felt you would profit then, and in years to come, from having a silent mother on that occasion. Besides, by the week's end your father had said quite enough for both of us!

Douglas, I so miss your folksy sense of humor and the daily ability to laugh at yourself. Our walls vibrated at your daily jollies, your zany advice to your brothers on how to become millionaires by twenty-nine (or get life imprisonment), and your side-splitting beauty tips for your not-so-longsuffering sister. Why, I can even smile and forgive you for bringing me those thirty-six pounds of ripe bananas on Thanksgiving Eve, knowing full well how much company we were expecting the next day.

"Mother, I'm home. Don't get shook up or kill me, but there's thirty-six pounds of very ripe bananas hiding your ham and turkey on the counter. I bet that's the most original one dollar gift anybody's unloaded on you. Besides, they threw in four pounds of ripe grapes, and you know me! I can't resist a bargain, especially food."

Despite your eating fifteen bananas that night, we were up at dawn delivering that monkey food about the neighborhood.

Your dad is missing your parading into our inner sanctum whatever the hour and booming, "I'm home!" As you proceeded to give us a blow-by-blow account of the evening's events ("I just spent $300 on coins and the president of the Clearwater Coin Club announced that the economy of Pinellas County will really take a downswing when I leave next week."), your dad would grumble good-naturedly "Douglas, go to bed! It's 1 A.M." Then he would mumble,

"Couldn't there be a little more of a communication gap around this place?"

Your sister, brothers, and grandmothers will miss your gift of a grateful heart. So appreciative were you of any small favor and you never considered it sissy or unmanly to express that gratitude in actions, words, or writing. You knew how to save for the very important and you knew how to give lavishly without counting the cost or expecting returns. Don't ever lose this gift.

We remember how proud you were of your early graduation gift—your first silk suit. You rushed to the store on your way to choir and presented yourself, in your gold creation, to your dairy manager for inspection. He raved at the sight of you. Upon learning that he had never owned a suit—he'd had to drop out of school and go to work in the coal mine to support his mother and brothers—you bent that six-foot-two-inch frame, put your arms around his frail shoulders, and announced, "Duval, my boy, I'm going to buy you a suit before I graduate from the Naval Academy! Furthermore, I'll even let you pick it out at the Army-Eagle-Navy Store."

All the employees at the store were overjoyed at your appointment. Many of them didn't know what or where Annapolis was. They just knew it was something great, and Doug, their boy, had made it! Such cheering when we rushed into the store with your official telegram. It's a wonder that all the eggs in the dairy case weren't broken or scrambled! You even had an application for chauffeur to Admiral Thrash that very afternoon.

Son, your Grandfather Cate would have been so proud of your insatiable thirst for knowledge. Doing your thing did not include mental inertia or even maintaining the status quo. A junior high math teacher used to groan, "Don't be so determined! Give up on those problems occasionally. You'll live longer." Eliminating nonessentials, you took the raw materials of an active mind and mixed, seasoned, and fermented theory with practicality until you came up with some real happenings! My heart went out to you in the ninth grade when a six-weeks *B* in physical education kept your name from being engraved on that all-*A* plaque in the office. Only one student attained that honor, but you never complained, or cried out, "Unfair!" You took it in your usual stride.

Your dad's farewell was a sheepish grin, choked by near tears, and the question, "Well, Son, now that you're leaving the family nest at seventeen, what advice do *you* have for an old father?" Your mother could say nothing, for with writing pad and shoe box of goodies in your hand, you looked like the poignant Norman Rockwell painting of the lad at the station bidding farewell to Dad before catching the college-bound train.

On this, your first July Fourth away from home, you realize, Son, freedom is not free, nor is it cheap. There are no bargain-basement prices. It's costly, it involves sacrifice, it demands Spartan attributes of self-discipline, dedication, loyalty, and honor.

Freedom is not the sole responsibility of any particular age group. The youngest signer of the Declaration of Independence was a mere eighteen; the eldest, Benjamin Franklin, had passed four score years. These blessings of liberty secured for us were not achieved by cynicism, negativism, or undisciplined behavior. These men laid the foundation and launched our great republic by looking far beyond their petty wills and whims. They possessed a vigorous, indestructible, all-consuming belief in Almighty God.

Your father and I have transmitted to you that same *living*, dynamic faith. Use it! Its resources are fathomless. "God in you" is an indestructible force!

Dear eldest, always remember you are "a little lower than the angels." Hang in there, Son! Roll with the punches! Go forth and bless others as you have blessed and delighted this grateful household.

P.S. Perchance, do they teach remedial handwriting at the Academy?

July 4, 1970

"DEAR FATHER"

Dear Father,
    I want you to know I think I have the best set of parents anyone could ask for. Although I've protested over the years, your judgment has always been best and there has been a purpose behind it. It may take me a month or so to see it but eventually I do see. I will always respect your judgment, and I know you will raise the others as well as you've raised me.

    I was really sorry to see the time come when I left although I didn't admit it. I began to cry the minute I got on that plane.

    I can hardly wait till Christmas when I can come home and I really *mean* HOME! I never looked at it as home more than I do now!

Love,

Doug

July, 1970—U.S. Naval Academy

CHRISTMAS HOMECOMING

Long before that big bird touched the terra firma and rolled to a halt at the St. Petersburg airport, First Son jumped up and down and yelled, "There's my mom! There's my mom! There's my mom! She's in red! She's in red!

Could this be the same son we sent away now striding toward us—straight as an arrow and two inches taller?

Douglas left a big hole in our hearts when he boarded a plane that June day as the loud speaker poured forth with *Gone with the Wind's* "Tara" theme. We choked back our tears in an effort to be brave. This zany prankster and consummate example of instant manhood made us wonder where the war was really being fought. Upon reading the Sunday chapel bulletin, his sister muttered, "Why in heaven's name do they have to pray that long prayer of confession. Shucks, they don't give them time there to do any sinning!"

Shouts of recognition, then bone-crushing bear hugs all around! Homeward now—our six, plus an additional four, to a midnight feast. "Make a joyful noise" was amplified to the rafters. The walls vibrated with music and laughter until 3 A.M.; then stillness, broken only by a faint rippling of the wind chimes.

"Isn't it great to have the nest full to overflowing again?" my otherness murmurs, half asleep.

Christmas homecoming. Our joy is not unlike that of those shepherds of earth when they met the angels of heaven outside Bethlehem in King David's pastures. What a memory to line the pocket of my soul!

"Don't be afraid. I bring you the most joyful news ever announced . . ." (Luke 2:10, TLB).

NEW HOME

Building a house is like being in the eye of a hurricane. You wouldn't have missed it for the world, but you don't have the energy to repeat the experience.

For too many years we've moved in and out of other people's designs. Nothing ever fit! We could have opened up a used drapery shop with our castoffs. Suffering through all those moves, we worked and reworked the plans of our someday dream house, incorporating desirable features from many of our abodes.

Then one day Daddy announced the time was ripe—it was now or never! (Actually we had no choice, for Daddy had already decided on the here and now.) Proudly he designed and then drew up the plans, overseeing the construction of our French country house—a five-bedroom, three-bath beige brick—nestled on an acre of eighty three oaks and pines near a university.

When the Master Carpenter advised us to sit down and count the cost before building, lest we end up with only the foundation, he gave wise counsel. Who among us ever ends up with the original estimate? We had no idea why our marble foyer exceeded the original price by $225 until we discovered the two "guest coat closets" had been marbled, along with a large under-the-stairwell storage closet!

On a humid July 7, we moved into our Thrash Taj Mahal on that Pensacola hilltop, along with the carpenters, air conditioning men, painters, carpet layers, plumbers, electricians, insulation men, three nests of mud daubers, and one demented snake who sought refuge from the blistering sun! What fleeting bit of lucidity was left after being cooped up three weeks in a three-room apartment self-destructed in that 94° heat and ear-splitting racket!

The temptation to roll over and play dead when the first

carpenter of the morn began his 6 A.M. St. Vitus dance on the doorbell was overwhelming.

Our younger males designed their upper-level attic retreat from their parents. The attic is furnished in "Early Barn" and "Later Boy." After helping Dad install a stereo wiring system until the wee hours of many mornings, plus coaching grass to breathe on this red clay and rearranging the entire yard every time someone gives Dad a new plant, they have declared their personal Declaration of Independence from another move. "We plan to be AWAY! At college, an academy, or RUN AWAY!"

Earth's crammed with heaven here in the country. Autumn's glow, pungent pines, orange berries, winter wind whistling over the hill, cardinals, blue jays, quail, and sparrows on tiptoe outside the family room, rabbits scampering noiselessly into the woods, squirrels playing hide-and-seek in the oaks, a mole digging his tunnel, the flash of a red fox, rain glistening like tiny diamonds on pine needles, and crackling dry logs in the fireplace leaping like shadow boxers.

Our twenty-eight-foot living room is furnished with a baby grand, stereo speakers, and huge pillows by the fireplace. That $1500 drapery estimate made us really appreciate those tall, picturesque pines outside our windows.

Our Taj Mahal has an active latchstring. College kids, service guys, and staff members add to our togetherness. The prophet's chamber is often occupied. All five bedrooms of the inn were filled with kin for Granny's weekend birthday party.

"Best birthday yet! We all ate so much we'll take turns pushing the car back to Meridian."

Spiced tea gurgles, candles trickle at twilight, roses glisten with dew, embers glow, and goodies disappear. Heaven and earth are near on our acre.

"Lord, I am overflowing with your blessings just as you have promised."

WHERE DID MY LITTLE GIRL GO?

We are four now. As the stereo station moaned "In the Still of the Night," Diane departed for Carson-Newman College this predawn August morning. All is dark in Egypt! Where did my little girl go?

Everyone told me it was easier the second time around. Well, it isn't. Sending an only daughter into the world is like an amputation—a limb being torn off. Never mind all that silly stuff I promised myself; I will graciously renounce my initial claims on my children, allowing them to make mistakes without a single "I told you so." That was before I began the renouncing!

"You know, she's just like her mother," my companion of many years twinkled. "Highly intelligent, stubborn as an East Tennessee mule, and always crusading for some cause." How dare he diagnose so accurately!

Such gentleness in her hands as she sponged my brow and patted my hand after all that surgery. Yet it was she who told her daddy, "I just can't go that first day. I'll hurt too much! Please don't expect me to, Daddy." But I heard her soft "Mama, Mama!" in that afternoon fog. She's carved from my heart.

And now my motherly heart is doing a flip-flop as daughter—dressed in jeans, patriotic sneakers, and that ridiculous T-shirt her daddy bought her in Underground Atlanta—stashes guitar and bed pillows atop that groaning, protesting heap.

And ole Mom, engine still idling from that major overhaul in her transmission, can't even navigate the driveway for a proper farewell. Oh, well, a share of my love and labor is gift-wrapped in your tuition. Your father and I have concluded that those responsible for affixing income tax deductions were raised by wolves, consumed only one meal a day, or thought orthodonture was a weed killer!

Go forth, my love and laughter daughter. Born clown with the "If thou hast two pennies . . . spend one for bread and with the other buy hyacinths for thy soul."

"I CAN'T PEN A POEM"

I'm afraid I'm not as gifted as you with your writing talents so I doubt I'll ever be able to write a poem or short story, but there is always one inside me about you!

Thank you for giving me life and thank you for the influence you've had on my life.

I hope you have a happy birthday and many, many more to come.

I love you, Mother,

Doug

(Penned on my Charlie Brown birthday card, March 14, 1973.)

MOM'S MONSTROSITY

Returning from an afternoon errand, I spied Mom's Monstrosity, as my family called that ridiculous glass candlestick fashioned from assorted bottles. Someone who eats regularly at our house had leaned his guitar too near that heap of glass, and both guitar and glass had toppled. All $6 worth of that turquoise candlestick was divided into five pieces and a few splinters.

Strange as it seemed, I chuckled out loud. I'd browbeaten my husband, against his better judgment, to get that object de art for me, even though he's made me carry that four-foot monstrosity through the streets of Atlanta to the parking lot. Carefully, we'd placed it in an army blanket for the 500-mile trip home. Improperly weighted, that candlestick's life span was definitely limited in our earthshaking household.

Going to my bedroom I hear muffled voices of concern. "Has Mama seen her Monstrosity? . . . Does she know 'bout it yet?" . . . "No, I don't think so, or we'd sure have known about it!" . . . "Sure hope she doesn't find out about it until after we eat!"

Calling the culprits, I inquired about what had happened. Of course, neither seemed to know. They'd spied the remains of ole Monstrosity a bit before I had.

"Oh, well! Nothing to get my blood pressure up to normal about. That thing was ill-fated in this household from the first. Losing my cool and getting superexcited about it won't bring it back!"

The culprits looked at me in disbelief. A dazzling smile of pure astonishment overtook David as he blurted out, "Good grief, Mother! I sure wish you'd learned that lesson a long time ago!"

"Take it easy on each other" is a cardinal rule of survival with our loved ones. "Of much more value is a man than a sheep." We major on the minors—allowing the huge amount of disposable junk that passes through our lives to usurp the real treasures. Forgive us for being overtaken with the tyranny of things and forgetting the value of a human relationship.

I ALMOST THREW IN THE TOWEL TODAY

. . . This twenty-hour-a-day grind is getting to me! If I could just have thirty minutes to myself on a bench somewhere to just sit. I haven't been to bed before 2 or 3 A.M. in so long. Tonight I was ready to throw in the towel. I almost called Father and told him I was quitting! Then I spied the old Plebe letter. Mother, I whipped it out and started reading it. First I began laughing, then crying. Henry came in and asked what in the world I was doing! I told him I was reading a letter my mom had sent to me in my Plebe year. He asked if he could read it. I said, "Sure! Why not?"

Well, after reading it, he said it was a classic—a literary masterpiece! He said I must be mighty proud to have such educated, intelligent parents. I told him I was. "I have a real smart mom, but she's so much more!"

And I took the girls' pictures out from under the glass of my desk and put your letter there so I can read it every day if I have to! I almost scratched out that Plebe and put youngster in its place. Thanks again and again, Mother.

I love you,

Doug

PRAYER FOR AN OVEREXTENDED SON

Father, this son of ours is overburdened with studying; he took too heavy a load, and it's fragmenting him. Gone is his joy of living and his spirit's almost crushed. He hasn't been to a ball game, seen a sunset, chased a pounding wave, sprinted to the rythm of spring rain, turned a somersault, or eyed a girl in so long!

Two of these killer courses could have, should have, waited another year. He wasn't quite ready. We tried to tell him but were silenced by his young logic. "I came here to get the finest education possible; I don't want any easy courses, even though they up the grade average and class standing. I realize my record won't look too hot, but I'm prepared to live with that decision." He never takes the easy way.

Father, help me now to resist the motherly temptation of "I tried to tell you." He knows this already with no prompting, no reminding from me. He must live with this overload and make the best of a bad situation. Help us to accept that, too.

Be very near him, Father. Help him to organize more efficiently. Brush the mental blocks from his tired brain. Revitalize his inquiring mind and revive his sagging spirit. Make him alert as he hits that fourth and fifth class of a very long day, no matter how many showers he has to take. He's going to win the Mr. Clean Award of '74. Above all, Father, make him realize he can't go it alone. He's trying too hard. Nudge him, remind him you're still here. If only he'd turn it over to you at the beginning before the burden becomes too much!

Restore his sense of humor. Remind him today of all the nutty things he said and did at home. Help him laugh at himself again. Don't let him take himself or his problems too seriously. Let him find someone in worse shape than he— that shouldn't be too hard at the Academy! Make him take time to worship, wonder, laugh, sprint, and live again.

Father, we love our sons, our daughter, but we can't hold on to them. We don't want to. They must be free to make mistakes. We made our share. I commit him and his predicament to you as these pink bands of dawn flame across the sky. Be with him today. Give him a five-dip, ice-cream-licking kind of day! Thank you for caring.

DRIVER'S LICENSE

Glory, glory hallelujah! I'm here at the highway patrol station on this 95° day with my caboose—the last of the line—on his sixteenth birthday.

I was here last year with his older brother. Now that was a real act of faith! The year before that it was his sister. She was a slow learner! Not really, we just put off driver's education as long as possible. How well I remember that day. A mile short of the boondocks, where said station was located, Diane declared she had forgotten her driving permit and birth certificate. It was 4:40 and the station closed at 5. I've relegated the memory of that next hour to the back burner of my medulla, hoping never to again conjure up the thought. When Mark and David extracted me from under the front seat, they added the "jolly" of the day. "We knew she was a hot-rodder, just like Grandmother!"

Was it my little Jewish professor who announced, "In America puberty rites center around the acquisition of a driver's license"? Having spent the afternoon at an exam station with his son, my professor looked a bit peaked. Well, to tell the truth, he looked downright ill! It was the only time our class lasted thirty minutes.

I wonder if my great grandfather suffered through his son's puberty rites. I can visualize him now. "Elisha Bain, must you always be the hot-rodder of the surrey set? Are you trying to find a quicker route to heaven than Elijah? Now you slow down to eight miles an hour before you wear out the horses!"

Dear children, as of this moment and with what precious sanity I have intact, I declare a lifetime moratorium on these puberty rites. I've had it! I refuse to ride with another child or grandchild to the driver's education station.

As my professor says, "Show me a floorboard with no

holes on the passenger's side, and I'll show you a car without teenage drivers."

LEARN TO NEST IN THE STORM

Were my motherly voice suddenly silenced and I were allowed only one capsule of advice to our offspring, it would consist of six words: Learn to nest in the storm!

The Master closed the greatest sermon on earth with, "When the storms come, the winds blow, the floods descend . . . ." He did not say *if*—he said *when*! Make no mistake; the winds will blow, the rains descend, and the floods surge. And they will mark your face, your hands, your soul. Who do you think you are to be spared?

It takes all kinds of weather to grow a soul. Radiant sunshine beaming blessings, rainy days that refresh and cleanse, snowy blasts of testing, and hard winds to break rotten branches and deposit debris.

Living is like licking honey off a thorn. You concentrate either on the honey or the thorn. Likewise, trouble never leaves you where it found you. You will sift and lift potential from it, thereby growing stronger, wiser, more mellow and patient, or grow bitter, cynical, disillusioned. Your attitude makes the difference.

How do you nest in the storm? By having deep roots! A fair-weather faith won't hold up; sand shifts with the winds of fortune. Deep roots come from an openness to heaven. The Master's secret has yet to be improved!

1. "In Touchness" with his Heavenly Father through prayer and a listening post (before any crises).
2. His second secret was an outgrowth of the first: "For I

have come down from heaven, not to do my own will, but the will of him who sent me" (John 6:38). You can never do better than make your will and God's will the same! Nor worse than living to have your own way. "If any man willeth to do . . . *he shall know.*"

3. Acceptance of the incongruities of life. God did not build a fence around his only Son and erect a KEEP OUT sign! Life isn't fair. With Jesus as your example you must be accepting of life. There is a difference between acceptance and resignation; one is positive, creative; the other negative, stoic, faithless, barren. Believe with unwavering confidence that he who regulates the elements, which are all at his disposal, will bring you through! Hereby lies active energy and heart peace of acceptance.

Lastly, ponder these amazing words the Master Healer spoke to a Roman army captain; they can change your life-style. "What you have believed has happened!" Jesus spoke this self-fulfilling prophecy long before psychologists latched on to it. If you think honey, honey it will be! If you concentrate on thorns, that will be! A positive mental attitude makes the difference.

There is no ceiling on a believer's dream. So get going; give life everything you've got and expect things to happen! What you believe has happened.

WILLY-NILLY NINETEEN!

A mischievous angel sprinkled joy dust on her bitsy bald head, wanderlust between her tiny toes, and wafted her earthward on the wings of a maverick—six weeks ahead of schedule. Our pediatrician handed her to us when she weighed but four-and-a-half pounds. "Take her home; she's rooted sores on her knees in the incubator. She's the most active preemie I've ever laid eyes on!" And so she has been a study in perpetual motion for nineteen years.

Like Paul of old, she's usually in the midst of a riot or a revival. She exuberates life, instigating excitement if none is about! Her brothers declare she invented collective bargaining. She collects on every bargain!

Impractical! During Ridgecrest staff days she wrote her father, "Please send me an umbrella from the store. It rains every day, and I simply cannot afford an umbrella on my salary." In her next paragraph she'd bought a purple stuffed pig with her waitress love offering!

What makes her tick? Audacity of imagination! As a preteen she came from church one noon reporting there were 1,267 squares in the ceiling. After a fatherly lecture about her secondary activities during the sermon, she reported the evening sermon verbatim with a postscript: "By the way, I was 1 off. There are 1,268 squares in that ceiling!"

Creative doubt, honest inquiry! "But, sir, I disagree . . ." Then she sets that superlative mind to computing and astounds her elders. Dogmas of the past are inadequate for her stormy present.

She's a gourmet of the moment. She radiates, "I'm alive!" She leaps into life and takes what comes—loving, suffering, agonizing, laughing, caring. She exuberates, cries, yearns, sighs, gloats, wallows! She has a love affair with life going! Eyeball confrontations with her are very disarming. "Aha! I see a faint crinkle of a grin to the left, which means you can't really be that mad! Yes, it's getting bigger and bigger!"

She has love in her heart and spurs in her heels. Such fervor for the underdog! To a high school teacher, "Could you please use the proper terms when referring to retarded children? You don't use the word idiot."

This daughter's liberated from status-seeking and the slavish desire to please status seekers. "I'll have you to know I'm too exclusive for your country club."

Unfortunately, she's her own worst enemy. Most of her disasters are self-inflicted. "I didn't think . . . ."

"Honey, what you can't keep in your head, you've got to take out at your heels."

She has an arrested case of common sense. "Oh, has it really been six weeks since I wrote? Well, no news is good news, they always say!"

She competes too fiercely! Her thing is most important, she thinks. Patience and gentleness of judgment are all too often lacking.

Frenzied activity is her lot; how hard it is for her to be still. Diane knows the world without far better than the world within. Inner solitude she fears. How she needs to be still and know! Silence has a meaning of its own, and inward voices still sing if she would but listen.

While we're hanging in there with our maverick, we wonder if somewhere our Lord might not have said, "Suffer the parents . . . ." It takes both Father and Mother clasping the reins of this spirited steed!

Every family deserves only one of these incredible creatures. As her father pants, "Diane will set the world on fire—one way or the other."

MIDDLESCENCE

Middle age. Right in the middle of everything! What unexpected treasure—this exciting Renaissance—the inward morning of the second half of life. What liberation to no longer be governed by ritual or reaction. What freedom just to be ourselves at last—no longer having to prove anything.

Middle age is a time of being realistic about limitations. It's acceptance of each other's trying aspects or no longer noticing them. We either do something about our habits or learn to live with them. Discarded, too, are impractical dreams with accompanying guilt and despair because those dreams were never realized.

Middle age is the maturity of seeing into the heart of many matters, having hopefully passed through the "lightning bug stage" of carrying our illumination behind. A time of perception, tenderness, a time of endearing openness, of rediscovery. Too little has been said about the beauty of love in the middle years of life. It's an atmosphere of love and living, family "ha-ha's" that need no explanation, an ease of long intimacy that's understood without words. It's coming back to the comfortable presence of each other at day's end. This occurs only after a profound tie of love, of commitment to each other.

Middle age is mellowness—the ripening years. Realization that our days are made of both good and bad. Mossy meadows and storm-swept seas make up our memories.

Middle age is finding our compass, reexamining our value systems. A time of asking how much money is enough. A time of enjoying the bounty of what we have instead of grasping for more. It's freedom from the tyranny of things.

Best of all, middle age is a realization of the eternal balance of things. It is a time of saying with the psalmist, "Keep me from paying attention to what is worthless!" It's discarding excess baggage and clinging only to the necessary with an attitude of profound calmness and inner quietness. It's realization of the congruity of God's actions to man's situations.

I am not dismayed by life's changing tapestry. "He has given me a new song to sing." New growth, new direction, a rebirth of joy! With the creativity of God in operation, there is no end to emerging life.

Middle age is what we make of it! *Carpe Diem.* Seize today! With no regrets.

WHEN YOU MARRY

Dear Offspring,

Though you are far from contemplating matrimony and I'm simply not up to becoming an in-law for a few more years, I will address the subject. By the time you take the leap, they may have put me away someplace!

My greatest piece of unsolicited advice came from an older brother, your Uncle Glenn, on his birthday shortly before my marriage. When twenty-two years later I mailed him that dog-eared, ink-stained epistle with a "You were so right" penned across it for his birthday, he responded with accustomed wit. "Why, I had no idea I was so perceptive in my youth!" May I share part of it with you?

". . . I hope you realize what a swell guy Willard is—sounds crazy, I know, for me to say that when you are going to marry him—but he is one of the most thoughtful and appreciative guys I've ever seen! His very open love for you, his solicitous attention and kindnesses—something few men have, unfortunately!

"I hope and pray you and Willard together have developed a companionable basis for a viable love—one which is small and young now, but which will be alive and growing. As you set out together, practice the words of Jesus, 'Love thy neighbor [husband-wife] as thyself,' with all it connotes and all that is implicit in this statement. If you can practice loving him as you do yourself and putting his interests and welfare on an equal basis with your own, I know he will meet you more than halfway.

"It sounds so simple and would lead to such bliss if a husband could always be putting his wife's interests first or at least equal with his own while she is 'knocking herself out' trying to do the same for him! But it seems we have too much selfishness and are too busy thinking of our own 'rights' to practice it too long! I've never seen this in a marriage, but I'd like to see you start and keep it up. Many start! But for some reason it never lasts.

"You have the choice and power to make a heaven on earth or in time the exact opposite for Willard—and for yourself. Now that I've given you this philosophical (?), foolish meddling, I shall attend to my own business. It may be foolish, but I'm holding out and looking for a chance to try out my own preaching, so will probably be your kids' bachelor unc."

Let me add to his masterpiece something from your own father, who had an uncanny talent for choosing the right mate. I overheard him telling a childhood buddy contemplating marriage, "Now, Francis, there are many girls you could conceivably marry and get along with. The secret is to find the one you can't get along without. Marry her and spend the rest of your life making her glad she chose you!"

Mom's pragmatic philosophy:

1. The Bible often says, "And it came to pass . . . ." Never, "It came to stay!" Remember that when all the kids have chicken pox at the same time, the budget's busted, it's rained for twenty-one days straight, and that grass in other pastures looks so much greener and the wind whispers of wanderlust! Hang in there and say over and over to yourself, "This, too, shall pass." It does.

2. Love never quits! The greatest gift you can give a son or daughter is to love each other openly. It's more caught than taught! Love is the greatest shock absorber of all. Let it put a halo on each day.

3. Trouble, properly aired and articulated, evaporates. Learn to disagree intelligently and houseclean your emotions.

(Sheepishly I quote your dad: "Stay on track. Don't muddle the issue by dragging in every misdemeanor of the last five years.") A Thrash translation of matchless Bible psychiatry, "Don't go to bed mad!"

4. Let there be spaces in your togetherness. Honor each other's self; allow it breathing space. Don't stifle the uniqueness that attracted each to the other. Perfect balance includes both interdependence and independence.

5. The minister said, 'Till death do you part," not debt. Be positively impulsive—on your anniversary only.

6. Let Christ umpire your home. The greatest cause of marital discord is ego domination—assertive thrust for one's supposed rights. Let Christ be umpire! He's the perfect arbiter.

P. S. All this works! Try it; you'll like it.

". . . and the greatest of these is love."

BROTHERS IN CHRIST

Dear Father,
Today is Father's Day and I'm sure it is the most meaningful Father's Day I have ever had (not that I'm a father—wanted to clear up my poor English). Today I went to a Southern Baptist Church in New London and they were finishing up a revival. Today I realized for the first time in a long time how I've taken my Christian family, that is headed by a fine Christian father, for granted. I guess it seems one reaches that age when he thinks he's too old to tell his father that he loves him. So many times I've heard, "When you're older, you will understand, and I always thought I'd have to be at least a hundred

before I understood and now I'm not even the ripe old age of twenty-one and I can say I understand everything and I thank you.

Thinking of all the children who have never heard their father pray or read the Bible, I know how fortunate I am. Besides having a father-son relationship we are also brothers in Christ and we will never be separated. How good it is to know that if anything should ever happen to us, we may spend a short time apart but we shall spend eternity together!

Like I said, it has been a most meaningful Father's Day and I thank you for all you have done. I regret I'm not at home to give you a big bear hug (I'm 200 lbs.) like I have given Mother so often! Take care.

Love,

Doug

Submarine School
June 17, 1973

MIDDLE SON'S GRADUATION

Taller and fairer than a Greek god, you march in your first graduation.
Mark, may you always be a learner—a student of life for life.

Eyes brimming with the blue of the sea, you've always seen the brighter side of life's dailies. "It could be worse! It might be Monday again!"

Hands as huge and strong as a Viking, you hold a dream, a scheme to realize that dream, and faith's beam to sustain and support your dream.

Swift and sure of feet—size 12's no less—you have a foundation of reality, practicality. "Could I borrow the family wheels Saturday night?" you ask on Thursday. "Bambi (or Grace or Mary—you give them all a chance) needs a couple of day's notice to get herself together!"

Here you come, graduation son, towering toward us—that impish, "canary-that-swallowed-the-cat" grin sprinkled across your countenance. How very proud we are! Middle son, neither the first nor last, but the frosting in between!

"Happy is the man with a level-headed son."

June 7, 1974

ANNAPOLIS, 1974

>Sleepy sailboats on the Severn
>Searing steeple of spun gold
>Stately Bancroft, ancient citadel
>Stained-glass Shepherd gathering sheep
>Ship suspended in celestial space
>Scion in black-marbled coffin
>Splattered statute of Tecumseh
>Solitary sentinel on an ivy wall
>Sacred scroll of the swords' fallen
>Scarlet dusk, shower-scented
>Strolling sweethearts clasping hands
>Shiny parades on grassy fields

Spouting cannons oozing smoke
Sloshers stirring a pool's reflection
Shower scrubbers at graduation's dawn
Scholarly procession of Academy sages
Spontaneous cheers for Mom, Sis
Sweeping 'copter bearing a President
Swelling intonations of "Impeach!"
Splendor of Old Glory unfurled
Soliloquy to scattering Blue, Gold
Solemn oath of commission
Spiraling hats recklessly abandoned
Starry-eyed brides, nuptial benedictions.

BLESS YOU, MY LOVE

Half the family graduating 1100 miles apart in six days!
We're pooped from "graduatitis" and chariot claustrophobias!

Bless you, My Love, for allowing me to be the last member of the graduating trio. Unlike those midshipmen, I didn't exactly scale the platform to receive my president's handshake, but my heart did somersaults of gratitude! Bless you:

For my "Thrash Scholarship" which enabled me to receive the first Education Specialist in Learning Disabilities from USF. (What a rapture to spend 52 hours in my field with nary a statistics course to cloud the horizon!) For your longevity of enduring: less than perfect meals, friendly household clutter, 4 A.M. study lights, clanking typewriter keys until 2 A.M., mislaid socks, and greatly delayed laundry service!

For your steadfast belief in me even when I doubted! You expected the best of me, and I was impelled to fulfill those expectations—stretching my capabilities to amazement at time. When I faltered, you encouraged my "I think I can, I think I can!"

For restoring balance and perspective to my muddled medulla with your frequent "Come on! I'm taking my top scholar out to dine. I have only 63 cents but maybe the money bags of our brood will float us a loan!"

Bless you, My Love, for honoring my dreams.

HOW CAN I KNOW?

"Mama, I'm awfully confused about all this 'God has a blueprint for your life' bit! Sometimes he seems so far away, I feel like sending up a flare to remind him I'm still down here at 4200-14th Way! How can I know what he wants me to do? I'm not one of those prophet men; God hasn't hit me with a two-by-four on the stroke of twelve! And how can I be sure it's something I want to do? What if it isn't?

Honest doubts from a very honest son. Is God practical? Will he ask me to do something for which I have no talent, no liking? Can I really trust him to do what is best for me?

Well, Son, most of us either inherit or latch onto the old Puritan idea that God takes all the fun out of life by requiring hard, stern, disagreeable, impossible things of us. They see the Holy Spirit not as Comforter but Accuser who makes us miserable, guilty, crabby from trying too hard, and keeps us and those about us from enjoying life.

Think back how many times we have heard someone mount the pulpit and wail, "I tried everything else and finally there was nothing left to do but give in to God!" Sounds about as exciting as standing in line to take a dose of castor oil! But Jesus came to fill our lives full to overflowing.

There can be no gifts without a giver. God is the Giver of all gifts. Would not the Giver know how you could best utilize his gifts? Would he ask you to do something without supplying the ability?

Another thing—you and I often say, "I just can't hold out!" We whiplash ourselves with, "If I could just do this or that, curb this bad habit, be thus and such." Forget it! We can't! So we prod on, bone weary, joyless, without direction. How foolish! Confess your helplessness. Ask him to do for you what you can't do for yourself. Believe he can, then let him! I think that's what "casting all your cares upon him" really means.

Now, how can you know since God hasn't used a two-by-four on you? Do you honestly want to know? "If you don't ask in faith, don't expect God to give you any solid answers," James warns. That's the secret! You supply the willingness and trust God to do the rest. Follow him one step at a time. You don't remember, but you learned to walk by walking, although you took many a spill. Just as you learned to walk by walking, you learn to follow by following—not arguing, doubting!

"Wear my yoke. It fits perfectly. And let me teach you." What marvelous simplicity! It tells you what to do, why, and how you are to do it.

What? Wear my yoke. Settle once and for all who's going to sit in the driver's seat and eliminate fear, anxiety, and the wavering indecision that dashes you to pieces. Hand over the reins or you'll muddle forever!

Why? It fits perfectly. What a promise! No more misfits. Troubles, yes—but he who gives you the day gives you the perfect ingredients for each day. Trust him and his superior knowledge which takes everything into account.

How? Let me teach you. His Holy Spirit will supply

mental energy, spiritual discernment, and physical resources from his inexhaustible reserve. Son, I know that! Commit your willingness to him, then meditate on his overcoming powers, not yours. Is anything too hard for God?

God's will for me has been everything I willed. At age nine I knew I'd be a teacher someday. I rounded up all the kids in the neighborhood and taught them on rainy days, whether they wanted to be taught or not! I knew I'd be a wife and mother of many boys someday, so I was never afflicted with "the old maid jitters." I don't find it the least bit strange that God who gave me these talents has provided abundant opportunities for utilizing them. Why, even when I was learning to swim like a fish and play every sport in tomboy fashion, I was preparing for a secondary career with handicapped children. When the time was ripe, God brought it about with no doing on my part. I just accepted the gift when it became available.

Eighteen months ago I asked for time to pen my pilgrimage. When three months later federal funding for my directorship ran out, I was tempted to whine, "Lord, this isn't what I had in mind when I asked for time!" Before I could mire down in self-pity, his Holy Spirit nudged me and said, "Did you really want time? Here it is. Don't question; don't argue. Get going."

Son, don't misunderstand. I hope I haven't oversimplified. Your daddy and I have been down on the count of ten—shut out on every side. It was so dark we even had to wait for hope. But our characters were forged on that anvil of challenge and crises. We didn't have a Pollyanna, saccharin-sweet faith; it was a long-term faith that saw God at the end of the tunnel. His "I will go with you all the way" was reality morning, noonday, and star times.

God wastes nothing. His gifts never fall apart, never wear out! They carry a lifetime guarantee. And yet we ask for a cupful when the ocean remains.

Learn to do by doing, Son. Wear his yoke. You can never do better for yourself. It fits perfectly. And let him teach you—one step, one day at a time.

"We confidently and joyfully look forward to actually becoming all that God had in mind for us to be."

BEYOND

As I draw together these variegated skeins of my spiritual pilgrimage of three and twenty years, I'm reminded of an experience in the oh-so-long-ago.

Diane, all of eight years old, was helping a neighbor hang out her daily ton of laundry. "You know, my mother will be so glad to get to heaven someday," our very grown-up-like daughter confided. "God is going to give her a new backbone, and Daddy won't be bringing home unexpected company every other night."

Having lived in seventeen abodes since marriage, this mother claims with reckless abandon His glorious promise, "Let not your heart be troubled . . . I go to get your room ready." Hallelujah! We who move so often joyfully anticipate no more moving vans, packers, cracked crockery, lost goods, damaged furniture, over-anxious offspring, and frazzled tempers. "When everything is ready, I will come and get you, so you will always be with me." Glory be! That's good enough for me. He will do all the getting ready—then come and get me.

How? I don't know; that's not my concern. He told us not to get all troubled about it. All we need do is trust Him! I rather think it will be like an experience during the young years of our household. Our children would chase June bugs or play so hard in the late afternoon or early evening, they would just crawl up on the couch after eating and poop out. Their daddy would gently scoop them up one-by-one in his strong arms and tenderly carry them to their own room, their own beds, where they would awaken the next morning, absolutely amazed at all that had transpired.

Being very much a child at heart, I believe my Savior will scoop me up and carry me through the door to my room in his Father's house. And I will awaken with no broken back—absolutely amazed at what has transpired!

So I do not await death. I await my Savior who never conducted a funeral but presided only over resurrections!

". . . I shall see God."